Tales from the Jayhawks' Hardwood

A Collection of the Greatest Kansas Basketball Stories Ever Told

By Mark Stallard

Sports Publishing L.L.C.
www.sportspublishingllc.com

Director of production: Susan M. Moyer
Project manager: Jim Henehan
Dust jacket design: Deana Merrill
Developmental editor: Erin Linden-Levy
Copy editor: Cindy McNew

ISBN: 1-58261-541-1

Printed in the United States of America

Sports Publishing L.L.C.
www.sportspublishingllc.com

To Dad,
my all-time favorite basketball coach.

Acknowledgments

All book projects require assistance from numerous sources, but this book in particular was reliant upon many, many people. First and foremost, many thanks to the former KU basketball players and coaches I interviewed: Adonis Jordan, Bob Billings, B. H. Born, Jeff Boschee, Nick Bradford, Greg Gurley, Tony Guy, Charlie Hoag, Delvey Lewis, Clyde Lovellette, Mike Maddox, Sam Miranda, Paul Mokeski, Roger Morningstar, Ted Owens, John Parker, Chris Piper, Kevin Pritchard, Dave Robisch, Otto Schnellbacher, Jo Jo White, and most of all, Bud Stallworth. Without these men and their recollections, this book wouldn't exist.

Mike Pearson, Joe Bannon Jr., Erin Linden-Levy, Jim Henehan, Deana Merrill, Cindy McNew and Scott Rauguth of Sports Publishing were terrific. Thanks for believing in the project and helping it become a reality.

Luan Billam's expert transcription skills were essential in the completion of the book–I can't thank her enough.

Barry Bunch, Ned Kehde and Kathleen Neeley at the University of Kansas Archives once again endured my questions and requests, and as always, were extremely helpful.

Sherry Williams, Kathy Lafferty, Sarah Goodwin Thiel, and Becky Schulte in the Spencer Research Library at the University of Kansas were helpful with the selection process for many of the photos in the book.

Keith Zimmerman and Matt Fulks provided imperative information for the book.

Finally, without the guidance and support of my wife, Merrie Jo, this book would not have been possible.

Author's Note

Anything that is more than 100 years old is going to have an intriguing history, especially something as vital and exciting as Kansas Jayhawks basketball. Arguably the best college program of all time–KU's rich history and tradition are second to none–Kansas's players, coaches and fans have long cherished the tradition of winning basketball started so many years ago by coaches William Hamilton and Forrest C. "Phog" Allen.

It is from that tradition this book was started, but it evolved into a different format, something better than what I had originally intended. Many of the KU basketball stories have been rehashed several times, and I wanted to find and share as many new accounts or recollections as I could. After interviewing more than 20 former Jayhawk players and coaches who were part of the program from 1943 to 2002, I felt a personal book, told from the players' and coaches' points of view, was more appropriate than simply rewriting their recollections and stories about KU basketball.

This is really their book, then, the men I talked with about their time as KU basketball players or coaches. There are other little tidbits and KU stories placed throughout the book, but more than 90 percent of the text is taken from my interviews, almost all conducted in 2002. Two interviews, with Ted Owens and Jo Jo White, were done in 1994. The few remaining items, unless otherwise noted, are from KU press conferences, the *Kansas City Star*, *Sports Illustrated*, *Phog Allen* by Blair Kerkhoff and the University of Kansas Archives.

Contents

Foreword

by Bud Stallworth

1972 All-American at the University of Kansas

In the summer of 1967, I was fortunate enough to have my parents send me to the University of Kansas Midwestern Music and Arts Camp to improve and enhance my trumpet playing. Little did I know or suspect that my trip to Lawrence, Kansas, would be a major event and greatly alter the path I had originally chosen for my life.

While at the camp, I also snuck in a little time on the basketball court. I had the opportunity to play against several Jayhawks players, including Jo Jo White, Roger Bohnenstiehl, Ron Franz, Vernon Vanoy, and Richard Bradshaw. I must have done pretty well in the pickup games, because Jo Jo thought I could play and quickly told KU coach Ted Owens about me. In no time at all, my counselor at the music camp got a phone call.

"There's a guy calling up here named Ted Owens," the counselor said to me. "He's looking for you." I thought I was in trouble.

"I didn't do it," I said. "I didn't trash the guy's room out."

"No, this guy's the head basketball coach here at the University of Kansas, and he wants you to give him a call." Funny thing, the counselor never did follow up about the trashed-out room.

Bud Stallworth (Lawrence Journal-World)

So I called the coach back.

"You know, some of my players have been coming over here talking about you," Coach Owens said, "and we've never heard of you. They think you can play at KU, and we'd like to know whether or not you have any interest in our program."

Talking about playing at KU was great, but I had to take care of more important business first.

"Well, Coach," I said, "don't tell my parents about me playing basketball. I'm here to improve my musical skills, and I'm taking a chance playing basketball. I might get hit in the mouth or something and then I'd really be in a mess."

Coach Owens assured me I wouldn't get in trouble.

"Why don't we talk to your parents," he said, "and maybe we can offer you a full scholarship to come out here and play basketball. Would they agree to something like that?"

"Sounds good to me." The prospect of playing basketball at KU was exciting, and after talking it over with my parents, I eventually told Coach Owens I'd become a Jayhawk.

And that was the beginning of my involvement with the University of Kansas basketball program.

I went home to Hartselle, Alabama, and had an excellent season my senior year in high school. I had offers from a lot of other schools, but I never wavered over my commitment to KU. One of the things that I really liked about the University of Kansas was its rich basketball tradition, as well as its academic opportunities. My parents were educators, and they definitely wanted me to go to a school that would provide the necessary tools to go on and make a difference in life and not to a place that prepared me for nothing more than the life of a professional athlete. KU was that place.

I think I must have been one of the easier recruits that they ever had at KU. One of the things I wanted was a chance to play for a national championship. At that time, UCLA was winning all the national championships, but I did get the opportunity at KU to play against them in the Final Four in 1971.

The basketball tradition at KU was just what I thought it was going to be, and today it's something that everybody in the country knows about. When you're a part of a highly successful program, working hard and leaving your mark means so much more when you're done.

Tales from the Jayhawks' Hardwood has many stories from Kansas basketball's glorious past, including a few more from my career. Extremely talented coaches, players, dedicated students and fans have added much to the legacy of the Jayhawks through the years. I'm very proud to be a part of that tradition.

This book is a slam dunk as far as I'm concerned, and I hope you enjoy it as much I did.

Bud Stallworth
July 2002

CHAPTER 1

Under the "Phog"
Dr. Forrest C. Allen

He is remembered as "the Father of Basketball Coaching," but to the University of Kansas, he *was* basketball. The outspoken, innovative Forrest C. "Phog" Allen coached at KU for 39 years (1907-09, 1919-56), winning 590 games against 219 losses. His many coaching accomplishments include winning or sharing 24 conference titles, spearheading the drive to include basketball in the Olympics, winning the 1952 NCAA championship, helping to found the National Basketball Coaches Association, and coaching 14 All-Americans. His 1922 and 1923 teams were retroactively named National Champions by the Helms Foundation.

Phog was elected to the Naismith Memorial Basketball Hall of Fame in 1959.

Otto Schnellbacher
(1942-43, 1945-48)

The "Double Threat from Sublette," Schnellbacher was a standout performer at Kansas in both basketball and football. A strong six-foot-three forward on the hardwood, "Snelly" hailed from the small western Kansas town of Sublette and is one of just three athletes to serve as captain for KU's football and basketball teams. He played on the great 1943 basketball team, which was undefeated in Big Six Conference play, and was an All-American in football in 1947. He scored 1,062 points in basketball for the Jayhawks.

I just thought Dr. Allen was a tremendous individual and coach. He talked about life as well as basketball. He talked about what we had to do when we got out of school–how to represent the University and how to conduct ourselves. He was a very compassionate man with his players, but he was also very firm and tough. He didn't take anything except excellence as a major, but at the same time, you knew when he was chewing you out that he loved you. He was not a mean man, but he was a very firm individual. He had his principles, and you lived by them or you weren't around. But all great coaches have that same ability. If you don't obey the rules, you don't survive.

He took care of us physically as well as mentally. He was very concerned about our health and our conduct, how we were doing in school. He made sure we were included; all the members of the teams were included–Roy Williams does the same thing–and you become a family. I really appreciated that because I was just a little ole boy from western Kansas. I had never been out of the state hardly, and suddenly, we're traveling and going all over the country.

Charlie Hoag (1950-52)

Another stellar two-sport athlete, Hoag came to KU from Oak Park, Illinois. He played in 45 games, averaged 4.4 points per game for his career, played on KU's 1952 national championship team, and was a member of the 1952 Olympic basketball team. A knee injury shortened his career in basketball and football.

Dr. Allen had experimental medical stuff. He recommended this machine for me when I hurt my knee. It was something revolutionary; I think it came from Europe or Germany, or something like that. I'm not even sure it was approved to be used in the United States. But he had me come over to his house–he had a little table and place in his basement–and I'd go over there and he tried to get my knee back in shape. The machine sent electricity through your legs in some way, and after he did it, it made the knee feel real good. For a while. But ultimately, he couldn't do anything for it. The problem was the ligament holding my knee–there wasn't anything there to keep it stable. So it didn't work out. But he attempted to help, and we'd go downstairs, sort of secretively. He was hopeful to get me back ready to play some basketball, because they didn't have a whole lot coming back for the 1952-53 season.

Clyde Lovellette (1949-52)

One of the Jayhawks' greatest all-time players, Clyde Lovellette was one of the most dominating players in the country during his time at Kansas. He led the conference in scoring all three years he played (1950-52), was a two-time consensus

All-American, led KU to the 1952 NCAA championship, and played on the 1952 Olympic team. Big Clyde played in 80 games for Kansas and finished his career with 1,979 points.

Coach Allen, to me, was a great psychologist. He could get you crying. He could get you mad. He could get you any way that he wanted to get you just by his tone of voice, by his mannerisms, by his eye contact. You had a father who could whip you with his eyes–Phog could do that. And on the other hand, you had a father who really loved you. He was going to make sure you knew what he said. And if you didn't, he was going to make sure that you understood the consequences, in his tone of voice, his mannerism and his eye contact. Now, as far as a basketball strategist, he knew what he wanted to accomplish and thought he had the guys who could accomplish his objectives. His thought was–for my class–to win the national championship and go to the Olympics in 1952. And we did that. He brought in a nucleus of guys; we all stayed together, we all worked three or four years together, and we graduated together. We were a family. He brought the guys together who could live and work and have fun, with no bickering going on whatsoever. I can't think of one time that the team ever got to the point of down times as far as a single player was concerned, like one guy getting the ball too much, or someone hogging the ball too much, or being babied by Phog.

I thought that Phog was next to my dad, and to be next to my dad, you had to be pretty tall. Phog was one of the guys that I really loved. When people try to tell me different things about Phog, I say, 'Please, I've got my own picture of Coach Allen, and I don't want you to distort

Phog Allen and Clyde Lovellette (*University of Kansas Archives*)

it by some innuendo or something that you thought, or something that somebody told you that is secondhand.' Until I would see it personally, he was aces with me. And for four years and after being in pro ball, he was still top-drawer as far as I was concerned.

He never lied to you. He told you the truth about anything that you wanted to find out about. If I was in trouble, he was the one who would tell me how to get out of trouble. He would tell me how to handle it when I owed somebody a bill. He would talk to me like a father. And he would chastise you, but it always had that love with it. You can be disciplined in the right way and you can be disciplined the wrong way. The wrong way is going to really hurt. The other way was the way he did it. You knew when you were wrong you were going to get it from Phog. He would chastise me just as well as he would chastise the number 13 player on the basketball team. He would send me to the dressing room just as quick as he would send the thirteenth ballplayer on our squad to the dressing room.

As far as Xs and Os, I'm not going to say he was the greatest basketball coach in the country at that time, because I didn't know anybody else. But he knew basketball, and he knew how to get the best out of a ballplayer. And I think one of the biggest things a coach can do, regardless of his players' talent level, is to get 100 percent or more out of those individuals. Do that, and you will be pretty successful.

Otto Schnellbacher

Coach Allen had control of us, and he knew where we were every minute. When I was a freshman, we had to scrimmage the varsity, and I had a good night against them. In fact, we beat the varsity in that scrimmage. Afterwards, I got a note to come in to see Coach Allen, and I thought, gosh, he's going to tell me how great I was and all that. I got there and he asked me how school was going, and I told him fine, I was going to class and passing. He just stopped then and kind of looked at me.

"Otto," he said, "you can do three things on this campus. You can play sports, go to school and chase women. You can do *two* of them well. Which two do you want to do well?" And I was thinking, "I'm not chasing any women." Then I remembered that I'd had a fraternity coke date recently.

"I know the answer, Dr. Allen," and I gave him the answer. He then asked me "Well, Miss Sweeder goes, doesn't she?" And I said, "Who?" He said, "Miss Sweeder." And I couldn't even think of her name for a moment. Then I said, "Well, she's gone." And he said, "I want you to call her up and tell her." I said, "I don't have a phone number." And he said, "Well, I do."

So he got command of me pretty quick. That was my freshman year, and from then on, the girls were gone.

I came to KU on a basketball scholarship, which included books and tuition. I did not intend to play football. I joined a fraternity because I could work in the fraternity at the tables, and I also got my room and board there. I could work at the KU job and make enough money to survive. I was working at the stadium, but then the stadium manager came to me and told me he had to fire me because I had a football job. So, I went to see Dr. Allen. He said, "Go out for football." That was the simple solution. That night I checked in and got a football uniform.

Charlie Hoag

Coach Allen didn't like Eastern basketball. He called them a bunch of alley ball players, and he thought they were crooked. We played St. Joe and St. John's the same year in the one trip back east. And of course we played St. John's in that championship game in 1952. It wasn't quite that bad. But they were pretty rough. You came out of a game with St. John's knowing they knocked you around, or tried to. It was a different game, and Coach Allen didn't like the way they played. Of course, they didn't like Phog Allen back in New York City. But I'll tell you one thing, he drew a crowd. When we landed, the reporters were all there to interview Phog Allen.

Dr. Allen was so outspoken. Everything was black and white with Phog. He either loved you or he hated you. And they didn't like Phog Allen back in the East. He didn't like the atmosphere, things that went on. We played a game against St. Joe, in Philadelphia, and they used to call a game different back in the East. Of course, we didn't know that. That was my first trip back there. I mean, they grabbed you, tripped you. This was in the first half. We were having a hell of a time with St. Joe, who was pretty good. It was really a rough game–they just played a different brand of basketball. At halftime, I remember Phog bringing us in and yelling at us and saying, "God dang it! Don't let those guys do those things to you. You're going to have to do the same thing to them that they are doing to you." And, I mean, tripping and grabbing and running under them. Somebody ran under Clyde and he came down on his back, and I thought the guy was dead. Phog got us to understand. So we got up, went out and started knocking them around. Not knocking them, but, you know, standing up to them. We ended up beating them.

Kansas State Rejection

Phog Allen in purple instead of the crimson and blue?

While employed at Warrensburg (MO) Teachers College in 1915, Dr. Allen applied for the vacant athletic director position at Kansas State. For unknown reasons, the K-State administrators passed on Allen and gave the job to C. G. Clevenger.

"[It] was the first time I didn't get a job I applied for," Allen said later. "Since then, whenever we play K-State, I try to prove to them that I might have been a success."

Phog's all-time record at KU against K-State *was* a success–73 wins, 26 losses.

B. H. Born (1951-54)

The slender center from Medicine Lodge, Kansas, stepped out of Clyde Lovellette's shadow in 1953 and led the Jayhawks back to the NCAA championship game. Born was the '53 tournament's Most Outstanding Player, even though KU lost to Indiana in the final. A first-team All-American in 1953, he also led the Jayhawks to a share of the Big Seven Conference title in 1954. Born played in 73 games and scored 918 points for Kansas.

Phog wouldn't go to Madison Square Garden. He thought the Garden was a bunch of jam orders and promoters. But one of my goals as a high school student was to play in Madison Square Garden. In those days, that was the really in thing to do. And, of course, I got to Kansas and Phog wouldn't have anything to do with the Garden. But then we won the NCAA in 1952 and had the Olympics playoff in New York with Peoria, the AAU team. We got to the Garden, and the Rangers were going to be playing there the next night. So they put the court down, and they put it on top of the ice. It wasn't very well insulated at that Garden. We were there the day after the circus had been there for a week. And my God, I don't know if you've ever tripped over elephant crap, but it was all over the place. They hadn't bothered to clean it up, and boy did it stink. And they had little light bulbs, like something Thomas Edison had hung up there–this is the old Garden now–those lights had only a half-block between them so you were in the dark most of the time. Went in the dressing room, except they really didn't have dressing rooms, they just had rooms where they had storage stuff. We went in where all these mats were stored and we had to actually dress in the hotel.

I didn't hardly get to play in the game because Clyde was in there. And then Clyde booted it, and then Caterpillar won the game in the final minutes. He missed a setup that would have won it for us.

Coach Allen smoked, but he didn't want anybody to know he smoked. Larry Davenport and I were supposed to meet him for some tickets at the Olympics in

B.H. Born, Phog Allen and Al Kelley (University of Kansas Archives)

1952. We saw him standing where we were supposed to meet him, and he was smoking. We didn't ever want to embarrass him, so we decided to let him finish that cigarette and then we'd get the tickets. Just as he finished it, he lit up another one. Now we're going to be late. And if you're going to be late when you're around Phog, you're in real trouble. So I said, "Come on. Let's go on up there."

Phog put the cigarette behind him. He held the cigarette in his left hand, and the tickets were in the left-hand pocket of his coat. He couldn't reach in and get the tickets with his right hand in his left-hand pocket. What does he do? He kind of stumbles and points over to something, and finally he snakes those two tickets out.

"By the way," he said then, "I want to give you a lecture on being late. You know, I've been standing here waiting for you boys to get here. Remember, promptness is like godliness." And he went through that whole bit. We finally got the tickets, but while he was saying this the smoke was curling up around his ears and behind his back.

Twelve-Foot Baskets

For the better part of his career, Phog Allen was convinced that the baskets used in college-level games should be raised from 10 feet to 12 feet. His theory was simple: higher baskets would neutralize tall players. His detractors were many and other supporters for the change virtually nonexistent.

At the start of the 1934-35 season, Allen's Jayhawks played a couple of games with 12-foot goals–which counted– against K-State. In addition to the higher goals, each basket was worth three points, and instead of two feet from the baseline, each goal was placed six feet from the baseline. The teams split the two games, K-State winning in Lawrence and KU winning in Manhattan. If anything, the two games were a convincing argument to keep the baskets at 10 feet. James Naismith watched the 12-foot action in Lawrence and didn't like the changes.

Still, Phog remained determined to get the baskets raised, and he continued his crusade well into his retirement years.

"The 12-foot basket is coming as sure as death and taxes," Allen wrote in 1949.

Clyde Lovellette

In practice, I knew I wanted to punish [B. H.] Born, and I knew I was playing hard against him. And I just made up mind that I didn't care how big you were, if you're going to go to take my place, then you better come and bring your lunch, because it's going to be an all-day job. I wanted to make a statement. And I think I made the statement, but one time I did too much and knocked him down.

Phog said, "I can't have that," and he sent me to the dressing room.

I could not understand why they forced him out as coach, because the man was in good shape. He hadn't lost his mind. He'd just recruited one of the biggest guys out of the East. I think Wilt Chamberlain would have stayed there for four years if Phog was still at the helm. And I believe that we could have won more national championships with Wilt if he was there. I thought it was terrible, a mandatory retirement. If a guy is in good shape and he can produce in your company, then why would you want to get rid of him? We talked about it. He was really down in the dumps about it. He thought he had a top squad coming in and he did. And then doing him like that after everything he had done for Kansas, and everything he'd done for the university. I could not figure out why the university didn't fight hard for him.

No More Booing?

In the summer of 1951, Phog Allen announced that the University of Kansas was going to start an extensive campaign to stop booing at KU's sporting events.

"To boo players in any sort of an athletic contest is morally wrong," Allen said. "It's time for somebody to take steps against it." Phog further explained his plan and feelings in the February, 1952 issue of *Household Magazine*:

"The boo is the twin brother to the Bronx cheer which emanates from the professional fight and wrestling rings. It has no place in high school or college sports. By indulging in this rowdy procedure, we have driven some of our best referees out of the business. It's surprising that some high schools and some colleges still have as many competent officials to work their games as they have.

"At the University of Kansas we are doing our best to replace boos with cheering. When a game is over, our players get together and give 15 rahs for the visiting team, win or lose . . . Our coaches and players try mightily to keep our seats and not to act like bench jockeys. We have tried to build a shrine against rowdyism to the memory of Dr. James Naismith, the inventor of basketball, who worked at KU throughout his long lifetime."

KU lettermen were supposedly going to teach the student body how to enjoy sports without booing the players. Allen felt the influence of varsity lettermen would steady rowdy students and effectively reduce–or eliminate–booing. Non-athletes, Allen noted, were usually the worst when it came to deriding athletes.

The "anti-boo" movement was a tribute to Dr. James Naismith and the value he placed on good sportsmanship.

Forrest C. "Phog" Allen (University of Kansas Archives)

Bob Billings (1956-59)

A western Kansas native, Bob Billings hailed from Russell and came to KU in the same class as Wilt Chamberlain. A member of the 1957 team that finished second in the nation, the five-foot-eleven guard had his most productive seasons in 1958 and 1959. Billings played in 65 games for the Jayhawks and scored 359 points.

Coach Allen was such a legendary figure at the time. We all just looked at him with reverence. He never let us down. He was a unique individual. You look at all the people that might have affected college basketball, you'd have to put him in the top two or three.

I think Coach Allen was very, very disappointed he was forced to retire. I know that Wilt [Chamberlain] was particularly disappointed, because one of the reasons he came here was the opportunity to play under Coach Allen. Although, in the latter stages of Coach Allen's coaching career, Dick Harp really did an awful lot of the on-court coaching. Coach Allen was only the emotional leader. Dick Harp did most of the technical things on the floor at practices. All of us were disappointed because Coach Allen thought that they would let him at least coach Wilt as long as he was here.

John Parker (1954-57)

One of the starting guards on the 1957 national runner-up squad, Parker averaged 4.8 points per game for his career. A heady player and good floor leader, he hailed from Mission, Kansas, and played for both Phog Allen and Dick Harp. Parker scored 325 total points and played in 68 games for the Jayhawks.

Dr. Allen was a tremendous motivator. He could inspire people to play beyond their normal capacity, and he was a great, great coach. In some ways, I think if he had been coaching us my senior year (1957), we would have won the national championship instead of losing by one point to North Carolina in the final game. But that's history.

Charlie Hoag

Phog was like 65 years old when I played at KU. He'd hit his head about three or four years before that, and while he still was a great organizer and a great motivator, to me the game was passing him by. He was trying to do the things when I first got there that he was doing back in 1930 or 1935. The old Hank Iba/Phog Allen type of offense, you couldn't win with it really, although they did. But it could be beaten. Phog made a great decision. He tried to hire Dick Harp, who would became the assistant basketball coach at Kansas. Dick was at William Jewell College, I believe, and he was committed to William Jewell. Phog never had an assistant coach until this time. Dick told him, "Well, Phog, I've got a contract with William Jewell, and I've got to coach there this particular year." Phog said, "I'll tell you what. If you come to Kansas next year, I won't hire anybody."

Now this is a story that Dick's wife told me and I'm sure it's true. Phog waited for Dick to come aboard the next year, and Dick Harp turned out to be very important to Kansas basketball and to Phog Allen. He was able to do some of the innovations, the little changes in defense, that Phog wasn't capable of doing.

The game had passed Phog by, really, is what happened. He was a great motivator, did great things for the University of Kansas, but he could not have won the national championship without Dick Harp. And that's a fact. I'm very strong about that, but I also realize the importance of Phog Allen.

Allen's "System"

P hog Allen was proud of his players who became coaches. In the February 1935 issue of *Country Gentlemen*, he wrote:

"There isn't an 'Allen System' in basketball in the sense that there is a Warner System and a Notre Dame System in football, but if you will pardon the pride, I want to mention that my players have gone out to high coaching positions—Nebraska, Stanford, Kentucky, Northwestern, Tulane, Iowa State, and to a host of smaller colleges and high schools."

Clyde Lovellette

Y ou know, the pregame talks he'd give were very quiet. I remember that. There was no ranting and raving. At halftime, if we were behind, he always told us "If you play the game that I teach, and you do what I say, win or lose I'll take all the blame. But if you go out there and you don't do what I say and play the way I want you to play and we lose and look bad, I am going to blast you in the paper. It is guaranteed that it will not be my fault, and it will be laid directly on you."

So that was sort of a motivation for us even before he'd start talking, because if we didn't do what he said, then we were going to get blasted in the papers, or blasted by him in person, and that wasn't for one day, that was for the entire week, the next ballgame. And it was continuous. Say if we played on Friday, and we didn't play again until the following Friday, it went on until we got ready to play. He hoped by that time that we were going to remember what we went through that whole week, and you didn't want to go through that again.

One thing that Phog sort of kept us in the dark about was the political wrangling and handling the newspaper people. He was going to be that for us. And he didn't like for us to make any kind of comments or explain anything unless he was there talking with us. So anything that went on as far as the newspapers were concerned or the selection committee was concerned, we were sort of oblivious to that. But the one thing I can remember is that I could not understand why we were selected to represent the conference in 1950 for the NCAA Tournament instead of Kansas State. I don't know if it was a political move or if something happened. I couldn't figure that out.

The Crusader

Never one to mince his words, Dr. Allen leveled harsh criticism on gambling activities and corruption in college athletics in the early 1950s. On the subject he wrote:

"The sad fact—sad especially for one who has fought for clean sports shoulder to shoulder with giants like Knute Rockne and Amos Alonzo Stagg and who warned his fellow coaches, as I did eight years ago, to clean house—is that athletics, college athletics, have been sold down the river. Last year's bribery and cribbing scandals showed how far the pollution of the horse parlor, the prize ring, and the numbers racket had been accepted into college sports, supposedly the citadel of sportsmanship, honor, and idealism."

Phog Allen with his "Phog Allen" basketball in 1928.
(University of Kansas Archives)

Otto Schnellbacher

The trip the team took in December of 1942–we went to Chicago and played DePaul and went to Buffalo and played St. Bonaventure, then went to New York and played Fordham, to Philadelphia and played St. Joe, then hit St. Louis and played St. Louis University–was probably the most memorable trip I took as a player, because that's when we jelled as a team. The lineup was settled, we found ourselves, and from then on we knew we were a good ball club. And we won all five games. That was during the war, remember. We stood up on a train many hours because the trains were full, and Phog would not allow us to sit down if a soldier was standing. I didn't mind that at all. It was a good trip.

Clyde Lovellette

When we went to New York, it was like 9/11—not before 9/11, but after 9/11. Security got tight. Phog wouldn't let us go to the bathroom by ourselves. He wouldn't let us move. And he talked all the time about this snake pit of basketball—he called New York the snake pit of basketball. He said, "You guys are never to be alone. You're with the trainer, Dean Nesmith, you're with Dick Harp or you're with myself or my son." If we saw something that even looked suspicious, we had to report to Phog. Even if someone came up to you and said, "Hi, how are you guys going to do tonight?" Coach Allen wanted to know about it. He was scared to death of the gamblers getting to us. And, you know, being a country boy, it would have scared me to death if someone would have come up to me and offered me money to shave points or throw a game.

CHAPTER 2

Teammates Remembered

KU has had many talented athletes play for its basketball program. It is the overall team concept, however, that has kept the Jayhawks at the top of the college basketball world. That ever-elusive ingredient, team chemistry, has always been a part of the Jayhawks' success. What was it like to play with Wilt Chamberlain, Darnell Valentine and Danny Manning, and how important were they to the Jayhawks winning? Jayhawk teammates share their recollections.

Bob Billings

You know, we never were in awe of Wilt [Chamberlain]. He was just one of us, did the things that we did. I had a tremendous number of classes with him, and we studied together a lot. I also roomed with him on the road. When we were freshmen and not able to play at

Wilt "The Stilt" Chamberlain (University of Kansas Archives)

the varsity level, we spent a lot of time together at practice and studying, classes and just hanging out like 18-year-old kids would. So I don't know if we were ever in awe of him other than what he could do physically, which was beyond belief. We'd never seen anything like that in our wildest dreams.

Wilt had, I guess, that negative image of not being a winner. Well, basketball's a team sport. If he had been in a sport where it was just an individual, he probably would have been the greatest in history and recognized as such because he would have beaten everybody. In basketball, it is a team game, a game that's coached. Look at the records and see how often his teams lost to Boston in the NBA in either the semifinals or the finals by one point in the seventh game. Now to me, that doesn't separate greatness from failure, especially when you realize he was losing to a team with a lot of players who ended up in the NBA Hall of Fame.

Clyde Lovellette

W ilt was probably the strongest man whom I ever played against. Now, I've got to say that I enjoyed playing against him in the NBA because there was a lot of motivation—mainly I was sorry to see him leave KU after two years. I didn't know the circumstances, but I thought it was terrible that he would leave Kansas and not stay his four years. I always kept that in the back of my mind when I got ready to play a game against him because it made it just a little sweeter if we'd defeat him. But you've got to realize that Chamberlain was 300 pounds and seven foot one and a quarter or something like that, and if you let him get a few feet from the basket, then forget about it. He was going to take you and the ball into the basket with him. He was just going to put you away.

He couldn't guard me outside, so I took him outside and shot. Of course, we didn't have the three-point shot then, but I would have done real well with it. We'd always put Bob Pettit inside or Cliff Hagan inside, and I'd take Wilt outside and we had a great run with him. I hated to play Bill Russell more than I did Chamberlain. Russell was quicker, a defensive ballplayer. Wilt, I enjoyed playing against him.

Chris Piper (1984-88)

Of the best-ever role players to wear KU's crimson and blue on the hardcourt, Piper's senior leadership and rebound-

ing skills were a major part of the Jayhawks' title drive in 1988. The six-foot-eight forward from Lawrence, Kansas was also on the 1986 Final Four team. An Academic All-Big Eight player in 1988, Piper grabbed 411 rebounds and scored 506 points for Kansas in his 129-game career.

D anny Manning is such a special player–those are Coach Brown's words–that he was, to me, one of the best all-time college players. When I broadcast games today, and other guys are talking about players, they'll ask about Danny. "You don't really think he was that good, do you?" The reason they probably say that is because his pro career wasn't as great as it should have been. He had knee surgeries. He got stuck with the Clippers, for God's sake.

Danny just controlled the game in college. He's six foot eleven, could bring the ball up and down the floor. A great, great passer, and could do every little thing, too. Danny would pick his moments every once in a while to rest, but he had to. He played 38 minutes a game and had to score most of the points. He was always so quiet, was a nice, great guy. Didn't have an ego. He didn't have to go out on the floor and score 40 points to be happy. In fact, Coach Brown had to make him, early in his career, be more assertive on offense. In 1986, one of the things Coach always got on him about was that he had to score. But Danny was so aware of Calvin [Thompson] and Ronnie [Kellog] and Greg [Dreiling] and that that was their team, so he kind of held himself back. That says a lot about Danny.

He was an All-American at Kansas three years in a row. He was one of a kind, there's no question about it. The game, the winning, was more important to him than any-thing else. He'd do anything to win. As a player, you knew that he was out there on the floor. You knew that he was going to make the play. Unfortunately, sometimes we relied too much on him to make all the plays. We didn't take enough pressure off of him.

Kevin Pritchard (1986-90)

The highly recruited Pritchard came to KU as one of Larry Brown's best signees, and he didn't disappoint. His position change to point guard midway through the 1988 season was one of the major catalysts that helped the Jayhawks run through the NCAA Tournament and become national champs. Pritchard was on the All-Big Eight team in 1990 and an Academic All-Big Eight selection three times. He played in 139 games for KU, scoring 1,692 points and pulling down 337 rebounds.

What does Danny Manning do well? He's a great passer. Shoots the ball pretty well, is a pretty good athlete. And he handles the ball well. But if you were to ask me what he does best, he makes his teammates better. Both defensively and offensively. Because he talks to you on defense. He's constantly out there coaching. He's just one of those special players who can do that, can make everybody around him better.

Bob Billings

As I look back on it, I kind of think my impressions of the 1957 NCAA Tournament are based more on what I've read than what actually happened. I do know that we were not able to stay in Dallas because of the discrimination at that time. We stayed outside of Dallas in a place called Grand Prairie. The crowds, certainly the SMU

Danny Manning (University of Kansas Archives)

crowd and the Oklahoma City University fans, were very hostile to Wilt and Maurice King. But when you're part of it, you don't really appreciate it as much as you do when you look back on it. It's kind of like our championship game. I've probably had a 100,000 people tell me that they were there to watch the last game with North Carolina. Well, Municipal Auditorium held less than 10,000, so they must have done it in shifts. But that's just how the legend builds up over time. It was a time when I'm sure that Wilt and King felt pressures that none of the rest of us really were aware of. And they handled it beautifully, never lost their cool. I remember after the Oklahoma City game, which was the Midwest final, a couple of their players came up and apologized to Wilt for the way the crowd had acted because they did throw pillows and some lighted pennies on the floor. It was a hostile environment for sure, but the effect on Wilt and King had to be much greater than on the rest of us.

Keep in mind, I'm 18 years old, Wilt is 18 years old. He was so much more mature than the rest of us because of his experiences growing up in Philadelphia and playing in the summer league in the Catskill Mountains. He'd had experience that we probably never had at that point. And he really handled himself beautifully.

He was one of the most caring individuals that I've ever seen. He would sit around and sign autographs for people. The prima donnas today think they are really put out if they spend an extra 15 minutes to sign autographs, and in fact, they don't do it for the most part. He was just a very caring person. He didn't want to hurt anybody on the court. He was so much more powerful than the people he was playing with that he couldn't afford to get mad. The only time I ever remember him getting mad was when Clyde Lovellette, one of my good friends and a KU alum, kept holding him when Clyde was playing for St. Louis and Wilt kept telling him, "Cut that out, cut that out." And then all of a sudden Wilt turned around and popped him, and the next thing Clyde knew, he was on the floor. Wilt could have lost his cool a lot of times and he just didn't. He just absolutely walked away from it.

The media attention was always on Wilt. For example, we went out to play the University of Washington in Seattle. Wilt and I had a suite in the hotel we stayed at—one of the rooms was set up for press interviews. The reporters would come and have all these questions to ask, and Wilt and I would be sitting there. And Wilt would say, "Do you want to answer that, Bob?" The attention we got—that Wilt got—was something unheard of at the time. Today, that setup would have been podunksville because the media we have today—well everything is just kind of geared for the media. The media back then, it was bigger on Wilt than it had ever been on a basketball player before.

B. H. Born

Clyde Lovellette and I averaged 30 points a game in 1952. Problem was, he had 28 and a half of those points a game. In those days, records were 30-35 points for some of the field houses. Sometimes I'd be sitting over there on the bench or over on the scorer's table waiting to get in, and they'd call me back because he was up around 35-36 points and they were going for the record. We both held the school record there for quite a while—44 points. Bud Stallworth ended up breaking it; in fact, I was there for that game in which he broke the record. He got 50 against Missouri one time when we had one of our reunions. He did a helluva job. Everything he shot went in. I got 44 against Colorado, which was a conference record. And Clyde, I think, got 44 against St. Louis.

D ean Smith and I were both on the team in 1953. We used to have to do work to get our scholarships. You got a bed, board, books and tuition, and $15 a month. Well, you had to do something to get that money. When they were passing out the jobs, they got down to the last two and it was between Dean and me as to who got which. He was a year ahead of me, so he got the first choice. He chose to coach the freshmen, be an assistant coach on the freshman team. The other job was handing out towels down in the locker room. So I guess I came within about two towels of being the coach at North Carolina.

Bob Billings

W ilt was a person who really didn't like to be recognized and honored. He didn't go back to Philadelphia to have his jersey retired for years and years. The only reason he finally went was because he had a very good friend when he was there, who was a trainer, and he was dying of cancer. He really went back to honor that gentleman, rather than to be recognized himself. He just was not one that was looking for any more glory. He had all the glory that he'd ever need.

Let me tell you, when he came back to Lawrence, he told me when we put him in the limo after spending two,

two and a half hours signing autographs for people after the game, "Bob, I've had a lot of good things happen to me in my life, but this is the greatest single day of my life." And he really meant it. I'm just glad that he was able to get back and was so warmly greeted by the crowds, most of whom had never seen him play because they were too young. He conducted himself as a gentleman, as he always did.

Tony Guy (1978-82)

The sharpshooting guard from Towson, Maryland, was a starter all four of his seasons at KU. At six foot six, Guy also played small forward, but he was at his best when he played at the shooting guard position. An academic All-Big Eight performer in 1982, Guy played in 117 games for the Jayhawks. He finished his career with 1,488 points scored and 415 rebounds.

I think that Darnell Valentine was a great basketball player, there's no doubt about it. But Darnell did not have a lot of confidence in the guys he was playing with. It was almost as if we had to prove to Darnell that we were worthy to be his teammates. I always found that interesting, in that you're talking about a guy who was a great athlete, but he was just an okay basketball player. I thought he was a great athlete, you couldn't help but admire him as an athlete. But as a basketball player, he was just an average shooter. If you look at the overall statistics, it's not like he lit the place up. He didn't pass the ball a whole lot, to be totally honest. I was a shooting guard, and trying to get the ball out of his hands was like pulling teeth. It was interesting because it was almost like we had to prove that we could play.

A rt Housey was a physical specimen unlike anybody I had ever seen before. That guy, by the end of the 1981 season, was in full bloom. But again you're talking about an evolution, and by year-end, he was a stud. He could flat-out play. My junior year was probably the best I had out of my four years at KU. I had a tremendous junior year. David Magley had a real good year, and John Crawford had a real good year. Booty Neal felt comfortable by then with his role as the sixth man coming in off the bench. He would come in and light it up. So all these ingredients were coming into form, and by the end of the year, we felt pretty good about ourselves. When we got to the tournament, we weren't intimidated by anybody, and a lot of that had to do with the schedule we played. We played an incredible schedule in 1981. We played North Carolina at Kemper Arena. We played Kentucky at Kentucky that year. And we played a number of schools that were really good basketball teams, so we weren't intimidated by anybody. We didn't have to be.

Paul Mokeski (1975-79)

A seven-foot-one native of Encino, California, Mokeski put together a solid career at Kansas. "Big Mo" fought injuries his first two seasons with the Jayhawks but finished strong, putting together solid back-to-back seasons his junior and senior years. He averaged 14.1 points per game his final season and

Darnell Valentine (*University of Kansas Archives*)

finished his career with 945 points scored and 680 rebounds. Mokeski played with six different teams in the NBA over 12 seasons.

Darnell [Valentine] came in as a high school All-American. He came in with a lot of hype, but I remember him as a solid player and a guy who was very mature and had leadership qualities even as a freshman. It's not easy to be a point guard as a freshman, and it's hard to be able to perform on the court and have a leadership quality about you that older guys who have been there will listen to. And he had that.

Ken Koenigs was my roommate for three years, and we're still close friends to this day. He was a six-foot-ten guy from Wichita–I was a guy a long way from home. He knew I was homesick. When it was Christmas or a long weekend or whatever, I'd travel with him to Wichita. Ken introduced me to some friends he already knew at school, and he tried to lead me by example by getting straight As and studying many, many hours a day. But I strayed too much. I was a B student. But Ken, he got one B in college and that was in freshman English. He was taking organic chemistry and all this stuff, and I'm taking–well, not the stuff he was.

I remember, especially my freshman year, how tired I was. Training had started and we were in conditioning class, then we had study hall and classes. I remember coming back from dinner and going up to the room for an hour to rest, and Ken's getting his books and going to the library to study. Then I'd go to study hall for two to three hours and come back. And he wouldn't be back yet. He'd get back at about midnight, and I'd be in bed asleep. He'd turn on the light at his desk and study for another hour before going to bed, then he'd get up for his early organic chemistry class. He was amazing. And he's a doctor now.

Mike Maddox (1987-91)

One of the top players for Roy Williams's first three teams, Maddox was an integral player on KU's 1991 Final Four squad. The six-foot-seven forward from Oklahoma City was also a

Mark Randall (Lawrence Journal-World)

member of the Jayhawks' 1988 NCAA Championship team. Maddox played in 123 games for Kansas, scored 946 points and grabbed 373 rebounds. He was also an Academic All-Big Eight selection in 1991.

Mark Randall was a great college basketball player. He got as much out of his talent and ability as anyone. He's six foot nine, probably weighs 240, and he's just extremely strong, did a great job of using his body. He was a pretty good shooter, and he and I worked pretty well together–our skills and talents complemented each other. I think Mark and I did about as good a job working together as anybody since Coach Williams has been here, of taking advantage of the high and low post opportunities. We were both pretty good outside shooters, so defenses couldn't sit back. They had to come out and play both of us on the floor, which opened things up inside.

Otto Schnellbacher

We had more than one person who could score on the 1943 team. We could score from the outside, plus we had great rebounding and defense from Charlie Black. Most of the teams did not score very many points on us. Back in those days, you know, we didn't have the 35-second clock. You hear everybody talk about the four-corner offense–that was our offense. We played four corners, and so did Oklahoma State. Phog called it, I don't know, transitional something. But it didn't make any difference what he called it, it was still two forwards and three people out, with everybody screening for everybody else. We'd keep the ball until somebody was open to shoot.

Black and [Ray] Evans were great athletes, and both of them were All-Americans. I thought when Charlie was playing and feeling well, that he was about as good a basketball player as I had seen. He would be great in today's game. Ray was a much better football player than he was a basketball player. But he was still a very good basketball player.

Otto Schnellbacher, Charlie Black and Ray Evans.
(University of Kansas Archives)

John Parker

Well, my sophomore and junior years, we weren't too good. We had a great player in Dallas Dobbs. My junior year, we were leading the conference, and then Dallas became ineligible because of grades. And so we went from first place to, I don't know, finishing fourth or fifth or something like that. He was an honorable mention All-American his senior year. We might have done a lot better had he stayed eligible. That is, we might have won the conference if he had been able to play the whole season, and you never know, because he was our top scorer.

Chris Piper

One of my favorite stories is about Mark Turgeon. Mark and I met each other in high school, played against each other once, and then played on the AAU team together afterwards. So we ended up moving in together during that summer before our freshman year at KU. After getting settled, we were supposed to meet with the strength coach, get set up for our workouts. Turg and I go in, sit down, and we start the meeting with the strength coach, who kind of looks at Mark a little funny. Mark, right then, was five foot ten, 130 pounds of braces. The coach keeps talking, and he keeps looking at Turg a little bit. He's telling me about the workout program–this is what we're going to do, blah, blah, blah. And the whole time, he's addressing me, telling me the schedule we're going to do. And looking at Turg in that funny way. At the end, the coach says, "Okay, great. You know what you need to do." I said, "Yeah, I've got an idea of what we need to do." Mark and I get up, and we're walking out the door and the coach says, "Oh, by the way, you can bring your little friend to the workouts if you want to."

"This is Mark Turgeon," I said. "He plays here." The coach didn't really believe me. So to this day, I always give Turg a hard time about it, because he was mad. Really mad.

"Well, I'm a player," Turgeon said to the coach. "I'm a player!"

The 1986 team was great. We had the best starting five, Archie Marshall coming off the bench, and then Turg as backup guard and I rounded out as the eighth guy. A great, great team. Calvin Thompson and Ron Kellogg were two of the best scorers in KU history. If we would have had a three-point line, Ron Kellogg would have been unbelievable. He had all those weekends in a row that he scored 30 or more points that year–they started calling him Mr.

Saturday, and that was without the three-point line. He was just an unbelievable shooter. And then, of course, we had Greg Dreiling inside. And then Danny Manning. Cedric Hunter was probably one of the most underrated point guards, I think, that KU has ever had. He was phenomenal and could really break everything down. We ran every play the right way, and we were great defensively. We had a lot of fun that year.

Tony Guy

Basketball was everything while I was at KU, yet it was still just a small piece of the puzzle. Dave Magley and I both understood that we were there to get an education. And you try not to think about those types of things because all it would do is add more pressure, and you'd be thinking "Hey, I've got to get this done, I've got to be a great player." We didn't need to add more pressure to that which already existed. Major college athletics is a big-time pressure cooker. I came in 1979 as McDonald's High School All-American. Magley comes in as Indiana's Mr. Basketball. Mark Snow comes in as a big-time player. We all come in together, we're all three great players. The following year I'm playing a big guard position, and they bring in Ricky Ross who was six foot seven and who was All-World. I'm going, "Well, where's Ricky going to play?"

"Ricky is going to play big guard, Tony."

"I thought I was supposed to be the big guard." I didn't get to play big guard until my junior year. It's not a coincidence that my junior year was my best year. My first two years I had to play small forward. If you don't perform, they're just going to recruit over you. I *was* performing, and they still recruited over me.

Chris Piper

When we lost Archie Marshall in 1988, Milt Newton came in and played the small forward spot, which was a good move. I didn't mind coming off the bench, and Milt was a better athlete than I was, a better scorer than I was. It was his time, so that was good for him. I finally got in the starting lineup when Marvin Branch became ineligible. So I went in at power forward. Mike Masucci was still on the outskirts here and there, coming and going, but he had his swan song, finally, and then he was off the team. From that point on, we really started to come together. Jeff Gueldner got into the lineup. We had a team that would play defense. We were the best defensive team that I played on, by far, because we knew we had to be good. We played hard. We'd work on–Coach had what's called a shell drill, a four-man defensive thing–and we'd work on it for an hour and a half to two hours a day, nonstop.

We got beat by K-State at home to break our long home-court winning streak, and we figured we were going to hear it really bad from Coach Brown. "Hey, guys," he said instead, "I see us turning the corner. You guys played hard, played great defense. They just hit shots. We're getting better." And then we got beat by Oklahoma at home again, and the crowd's booing us and stuff. And he's, "No, you guys are getting better." Then we went down to Missouri and beat them. By then that team really felt like it was a good team. The record didn't show it, but we felt like we could play with anybody.

Milt Newton (University of Kansas Archives)

Bud Stallworth (1969-72)

The slick-shooting six-foot-five guard from Hartselle, Alabama, never saw a shot he didn't like, and that was good for the Jayhawks. Bud Stallworth unloaded long jump shots from all over the court for most of his career, and when he was hot, KU usually won. He was selected for the All-Big Eight Conference team twice, named Big Eight Player of the Year in 1972, an All-American in 1972, and an Academic All-American in 1971. Stallworth averaged 25.3 points per game in 1972–his senior season–played in 82 games, and finished his career with 1,495 points.

I grew up watching the Globetrotters and the predominantly black colleges. They'd warm up to

"Sweet Georgia Brown," and I picked up their moves and copied what they were doing. All of us did in Alabama. So I had a little talent for the fancy moves when I got to KU.

The first time I did that at Kansas–dribbling between my legs and going behind the back–I caught hell.

"Oh, no, no, no, no," Sam Miranda, one of our assistant coaches, yelled. "Wait a minute. What are you all doing? We don't do that here. We don't do that fancy stuff here. We do the basic fundamentals." I was surprised. They didn't tell me when they were recruiting me that I was going to play a real conservative kind of game.

My sophomore year started out well, but as the year got on, I probably got a little more liberal with my approach. I liked to shoot 20-foot jump shots, sometimes 30-foot jump shots, but KU's basketball philosophy was to get the ball to the big guy, and if they couldn't get it close to the basket and score, then you took the second and third option and shot that jump shot. And they don't want a 20-footer, they wanted a 12- to 15-footer. But we had Dave Robisch, who was our leading scorer. So I had to kind of temper my game to fit in with the team. I wasn't progressing fast enough, I guess, for Coach Owens to keep on letting me be out there with them. So he sat me down, pulled me out of the starting lineup, probably the last five or six games of my sophomore year. That made me a little angry. It wasn't that I thought I was the best player, but it set me back and bruised my ego.

A lot of things were happening while I was at KU. The Vietnam thing was going on, there was a lot of racial stuff in Lawrence, and a local kid was killed by the police. The National Guard came to the campus. They bombed the military science building; they burned the student union. The black athletes at KU were caught in the middle of all that.

And they didn't have a black cheerleader. The administration had all these reasons why there wasn't a black cheerleader. The black student union came to us, the black athletes, and asked for our support.

"We need you to boycott practice," we were told. "You need to tell the coach you're not going to play if you don't have a black cheerleader."

I'm out here trying to get a degree and trying to play basketball. There was no way I was going to boycott practice. I told them if they wanted to give me my scholarship money, then maybe I'd think about it. They ended up, I think it was my senior year, finally getting a black cheerleader.

Roger Morningstar

A junior college transfer, Morningstar made the most of his two seasons at KU. He played on the 1974 Final Four team and helped the Jayhawks win the Big Eight twice, in 1974 and 1975. The six-foot-six forward from Dundee, Illinois played in 55 games for Kansas, scoring 645 points.

We were a prototypical team in 1974. We had Rick Suttle, who that year was probably our best player. Big, six-foot-ten kid who could do a lot of things—shoot the ball pretty well from outside, a good rebounder, had a lot of energy, and had his own kind of little spirit thing going. Danny Knight was a big, six-foot-ten kid who was kind of a plodder. He wasn't real quick, just a big, burly guy, but was very effective underneath. And then Dale Greenlee was an incredible shooter. Tom Kivisto was not only a good team leader, he was a good ball handler who sacrificed a lot of his ability to score by getting the ball to some of the rest of us to shoot. We didn't have any great players, but we had the ability to make the talent that we had work to the best of its abilities. So that was kind of fun. It's taught me a lot in life, after basketball, what it means to sacrifice individually for the good of the team. And that kind of enables you to look at things in a little different perspective than maybe just win-win-win-win-win. It was a pretty cool experience. It's fun to be successful when it's like that. It's fun to share that with a group of guys, and we've remained close over the years for the most part.

Bud Stallworth

Dave Robisch had to be motivated. If you roll me out in the gym today to play a pickup game, I'm going to play as hard as I can play. That's just the way I am. Some guys, you roll them out in practice, they're not going to do it. They play hard or harder in a game environment than they do in practice because they figure, I don't need to be doing that little extra sprint when I can do this little trot. And Dave was that kind of guy. He could shoot, he was big, and even though it didn't look like it, he could move and score. Every now and then he would do something lazy in practice, throw a bad pass or not block out to get the rebound. And if somebody said something to him, he'd make a little comment. And Coach Miranda would send him up in the bleachers. He wouldn't even hesitate. That was the punishment, running up and down the bleachers. That's just the way Dave was, but he showed up for every game.

Roger Brown, Dave Robisch and Pierre Russell celebrate after the Jayhawks win the 1971 NCAA Midwest Regional. (Lawrence Journal-World)

In 1971, we lived like a family–Roger Brown, Pierre Russell, Robisch, Aubrey Nash and me. If you saw one of us, 60 to 70 percent of the time, you saw all five of us. We were the starting five my junior year. We lived on the same floor. If Dave wasn't with us, it's probably because he was with his future wife. And she would be with us, too. And that's just the way it was. Pierre, Roger, Aubrey and I, we probably spent more time together than most families in Lawrence, Kansas, for three years. We just hung out together. And we were successful. We had a good chemistry. You don't get any farther than playing for the national championship and being in the Final Four. If you do that in college basketball, you've accomplished something. I thought it was a lot easier to win a championship because UCLA was always doing it. I thought, "Well, shoot, I can go out to KU and at least play in a couple Final Fours, maybe win one." Now that I'm older, I see that many great teams don't even get out of the regionals. We had to win our conference to get a chance to dance. I tell people all the time that it's a little watered down now. You can get lucky and get into at least the finals of a regional now because there are so many teams coming in, or you can get unlucky and get knocked out by a team that had a hot night.

CHAPTER 3

Holding the Tradition

Ted Owens

The fifth head coach in the history of Kansas basketball, Ted Owens directed the Jayhawks for 19 seasons from 1964 through 1983. His record speaks for itself: 348 wins at KU, six conference titles, seven trips to the NCAA Tournament, and two Final Four appearances–1971 and 1974. Five All-Americans played for him, and his 1968 team took second place in the NIT. Owens was Big Eight Coach of the Year five times, and he was named the National Coach of the Year in 1978.

Dave Robisch (1968-71)

One of the premier players in the history of KU basketball, Robisch came to Lawrence as a much ballyhooed and sought-after recruit. He lived up to his promise and more. The big, six-foot-ten forward from Springfield, Illinois, garnered many individual awards during his career: First team All-American in 1971, All-Big Eight three years in a row, and twice–in 1970 and 1971–he was named Big Eight Player of the Year. Robisch played in 83 games for KU, scored 1,754 points–an average of 21.1 points per game–and grabbed 815 rebounds.

We were getting ready to start Big Eight conference play after we had finished our preseason schedule–we had won the Big Eight tournament and had only lost one game. Coach Owens and Coach Catlett called me into the office, and they pretty much said that they knew I'd been struggling shooting a little bit in the preseason schedule, but still we had lost only one game and were ranked in the top five in the country. They said they thought that I could play better and that if we didn't win the Big Eight, it was all on my shoulders.

With Coach Owens, it was a love-hate relationship at times, but that was part of the psyche of getting me motivated. He always accused me, along with Ron Franz, of being one of the worst practice players that he ever had in his coaching career at KU. My response was usually, "Well, Coach, whatever." He used that as a motivational tool, but I'll be forever grateful. His assistants, Coach

Dave Robisch (University of Kansas Archives)

Catlett and Coach Miranda, worked with me from the first day that I got on campus as a freshman. Particularly Coach Miranda and his individual drills. He was with me every day from the time I was a freshman until the time that I left. So, I was forever grateful to them.

I felt our sophomore year, if Jo Jo White would have been able to stay in school the second semester, that we would have had a great chance to go to the Final Four. Without his leadership, the rest of the team wasn't ready for that situation. Yet I felt that I played pretty well as a sophomore, but to lose him in midyear was something we couldn't recover from. And we were ranked in the top five in the country when he left.

Roger Morningstar

I don't think there's any coaching staff that will ever sit in their office and say, "You know what? We're in trouble, and we're not going to win a game." For the most part, I think coaches are optimistic people. And what Coach Owens had in 1974 was a bunch of pieces. I think they had what they felt was quite a bit of talent, even the year before I got here when they were eight and 20 or whatever it was. They had Rick Suttle and Danny Knight and Dale Greenlee, Tommy Smith, Tom Kivisto—there were a lot of pieces there. It was kind of a chemistry thing. They were missing something. Norman Cook came in out of high school the same year that I came in. Norman, of course, was an incredible talent. A six-foot-eight kid who could do a bunch of things. I think with him, the coaches saw something could happen. But I'll tell you, it didn't come real easy.

We started off the season, and we were playing okay. We went over to what was then the Big Eight preseason tournament in Kansas City. It was played that year at Municipal Auditorium, the last year they played there. That tournament was always a lot of fun, as the Big 12 postseason tournament is now. We lost to Colorado in a pretty close game. They weren't as bad as we might have thought they were, but we lost and didn't feel like things just went real well. So we had a big team meeting, and, of course, I'm just happy to be at Kansas. I'm not looking to stir anything up because I haven't been there long enough, paid my dues or any of that kind of stuff as of yet. We aired some things out, and I had to give it to the coaching staff–Coach Reid, Coach Miranda and our head coach, Ted Owens. They had the wherewithal to listen and not just totally agree, but just shake their heads and say, "You know what? We'll try. We'll try and open it up a little bit." They kind of listened and loosened it up a little bit, and from that point on, we went on a run.

We only lost one conference game in 1974, and once we got some momentum going, we were able to sneak into the Final Four. We had one other game that was kind of a tell-tale, too. It was against Vanderbilt, and we went down there. They thumped us pretty good. I remember coming back, we left very early the next morning from Nashville and flew back into KC. Then we got on a bus and drove back to Lawrence. But instead of pulling up to Jayhawk Towers like we normally did, the bus went right by the Towers and pulled into the back of Allen Fieldhouse. And Coach Owens said, "You've got ten minutes to get dressed and get your butts out on the floor."

We went for about four or four and a half hours. There wasn't a whole lot of basketball involved, and what basketball was involved was more like the WWF with some sprints in between. A little bit like a war. That might have been our first wake-up call as to them thinking, "We've got the ingredients here to have a pretty good team, and until you guys start figuring it out, you know what? We're not going to treat you very normal."

Paul Mokeski

I know Coach Owens had a great coaching career at Kansas. He did a great job recruiting and bringing players along. I don't know what his graduation rate was, but I think it was pretty high. He expected you to go to class. He expected you to graduate on time if at all possible.

My relationship with him was kind of in between, but it wasn't distant by any means. He was a coach who would invite the whole team over for Christmas breakfast or before the season started. You worked the summer camps, you got to know him a little bit more during the summer camp when it was more laid-back. During the season, he was pretty high-pressure and under pressure. He was pretty intense.

What usually happens is that players–college or pro level–get to know their assistant coach more than their head coach. It's just the nature of the beast. I think it was the same way back then. I knew he cared about us. He cared about me. He cared about his players. I wasn't afraid to knock on his door and ask him questions, whether they were about school, life or basketball. And I knew he would tell me the truth.

Tony Guy

Coach Owens didn't scream a whole lot. I think that had to do with the fact that Darnell [Valentine] was running the show. Darnell pretty much knew what

Ted Owens (Lawrence Journal-World)

needed to be done, and he was in control. There wasn't much Coach Owens needed to say. That's one of the advantages of having a veteran leader. You don't have to do a lot of screaming and yelling. Practice was a lot of fun, but it would also get intense.

Roger Morningstar

There needs to be a chemistry in a coaching staff to make things work well. We used to call Coach Owens–kind of behind his back–"Smiling Ted." He just wasn't a very good "mean" person. And everybody, after we kind of tried to feel our oats and see how far we could push things–everybody kind of settled into this respect thing and knew that the coaches knew what they were talking about. Coach Owens just had–we laugh about it today–a hard time being mean. He was just too nice a guy. He wasn't a good "mean" person. Coach Owens knew Xs and Os, and he knew what we needed to do, and he was good about that.

Then we had Coach Miranda, who was a drill sergeant. There wasn't one of us who wasn't scared to death to look at him cross-eyed, because that's just the way he was. He was a strict disciplinarian–no nonsense, no jacking around. Nothing. We thought he was mean back then, but that combination with Coach Owens really worked well together. And then Coach Duncan Reid–we didn't see a lot of Coach Reid, because in those days, you could recruit 365 days a year–he'd be out on the road recruiting during much of the season. But he was also a tough guy who grew up in Chicago as a kid. There was no nonsense with him. He'd get in your face and grab you and push you around. That's just kind of the way it was back then. Actually, we all enjoyed that. We look back on it now and it's maybe one of the things that kids are missing in today's society. There's just not a whole lot of discipline with some of these kids and just not a lot going on at home. They were a tough coaching staff, but there was just enough of a "little nice guy" in there, especially from Coach Owens, to kind of break the ice. So there was a nice chemistry there with the coaches.

Tony Guy

We knew what we had to do in practice. We had Lafayette Norwood and Bob Hill for assistant coaches, and they were excellent at practice. Coach Hill was a technician who could break the game down. One of the reasons I got better at KU was because of Bob Hill and his understanding of the fundamentals of the game. You look at so many college players today who don't get better. They're in school for four years, and they don't get better. You look at these great athletes who are not fundamentally sound. They are poor, poor basketball players. They just happen to be pretty good athletes. At KU a lot of guys got better. It was because Coach Norwood and Coach Hill were technicians. Coach Owens was the CEO. He knew what we needed to do and that sort of thing, but Coach Hill and Lafayette prepared us offensively and defensively to be successful on the basketball court.

Bud Stallworth

Jo Jo White was doing Coach Owens's camp, and I worked out with him on a daily basis, talked to him a little bit about the things that he thought I needed to work on. Another guy came back to Kansas who had played here, Al Lopes, who is now an attorney in Lawrence. Al pulled me aside one day and said, "If you don't change the way you're acting around here, they're going to get rid of you."

"What are you talking about?"

"You're a high-profile kind of an individual here," Lopes said. "You're on the KU basketball team, and even though this isn't the South, maybe you need to change some of your social activities."

"Are you talking about the ladies that I'm going out with? Is that the problem? Break it down for me." He told me to figure it out. So I was going to school, not skipping classes, and I was playing basketball. What else did I need to do? I was doing all the right things, but there was still a little friction going on.

Bud Stallworth (Lawrence Journal-World)

It was that there was some friction about black players dating white girls, even in Lawrence, Kansas. That was the reality of it all. I don't know for sure if that was the problem or not, and Coach Owens never came to me and said that's what it was, but it may have been some alumni that had a daughter here that maybe made a comment about it. I don't know. All I know is that it's not about just going out and playing basketball sometimes.

Coach Owens was the recruiter type. He was the guy who could talk to the parents and then pull everything together for the game. Sam Miranda was the enforcer. He was the marine; the "Little Napoleon", we used to call him. And Coach Catlett was like the uncle, the guy we could go to if we were hungry or wanted to go to the movies. You know, can we borrow a car? He was that kind of guy. He could talk our language a little bit. He wasn't in the authoritative role thing.

Coach Owens was the head coach, so you couldn't joke around with him. Miranda didn't want you thinking about joking around with him. He made sure that you knew that he was the man, and if you screwed up, he wanted to make sure you remembered it. So you wanted to stay on his good side most of the time. Coach Owens was like the CEO. He was the guy that if you failed, it was resting on his shoulders. He was the guy that had to put it together and make it work. And everybody else had to make sure they were in their place to do that. I thought he did a pretty good job of it. I look back now and some of the things he was trying to get me to do probably helped me along the way, and if I had been too bull-headed and not listened, I probably wouldn't have made it through here. He had his guidelines that he wanted us to follow, and when you make a commitment to a school, you make a commitment to follow the rules, whatever they might be.

Dave Robisch

My sophomore year, we were the first team that went from the red road uniforms to the blue. I can't remember what the decision was; I guess Coach Owens wanted a change, or the school did. I do remember the old red uniforms had the belt buckle in the middle. My sophomore year was the first year that we went to elastic belt with the drawstring instead of having that belt. I thought that belt was pretty damn ugly, and I was glad to get rid of those uniforms.

Everybody today remembers how short the uniform pants were back in those days. They all wear them around their knees now, below their knees if they can get away with it. A lot of times they look at the uniforms we played in and kind of laugh because they were pretty short, but that's just because that's the way we grew up. We didn't think anything about it.

Ted Owens Fired

After two consecutive losing seasons in 1982 and 1983, Ted Owens was fired. At the KU basketball banquet that year, he spoke publicly—with a lot of emotion—about his firing for the first time.

"I won't say I don't have anger and bitterness. It comes and goes. I am so disappointed I won't have a chance to work with this bunch next year.

"Only history will determine what kind of career we had here. I don't know who will be the new coach here, but no one could love this place more than me."

CHAPTER 4

Recruiting Tales

Recruiting student athletes has been a hard-nosed, cutthroat business in college athletics for decades. It's a process that has become necessary, and the Jayhawks have nabbed more than their share of top prospects. But why did some players select Kansas over other schools, and why did KU stand out more than other programs? Some players didn't pick KU, a few recruits performed better than expected, and a couple were lucky to end up on the University of Kansas campus at all. Here are the reasons some players came to the University of Kansas to play basketball.

Otto Schnellbacher

I visited Kansas State, and I had a hard time getting away from them. They didn't listen to me when I said, "No, I want to go see KU." I called Coach Allen from K-State and said, "Hey, I'm going to have a hard time getting away from here. I'm going to catch a late night bus and

I'll be in Lawrence about one o'clock." Phog said he'd meet me, and he did. I immediately liked him, and from the time that I met him, I knew that's where I was going to go to school if he would take me. Phog Allen was the real reason I went to KU.

B. H. Born

The K-State coach, Jack Gardner, called me, so I went up to Manhattan to this dinner. After the dinner, he said, "Let's go over to the president's office." We went over to Dr. Eisenhower's office–he was head of the school, and he was President Eisenhower's brother. We were sitting there, and he said, "B. H., why don't you go ahead and say you're coming to K-State and get all this tension off so you can finish the year? Then you won't have to worry about all these recruiting trips." I nicely told him that I hadn't made my mind up yet where I was going to go and what I was going to do. They were not happy with me.

Chris Piper

I got extremely lucky. I wasn't recruited by any major Division I programs. I was recruited by most of the NAIA schools and junior colleges in Kansas. I had come down to trying to make a decision between going and playing NAIA basketball at Washburn or going and playing for a junior college at Hutchinson or Dodge City and trying to go to Division I after that. I really had no idea what I wanted to do. All of a sudden, my high school coach tells me that Coach Brown wanted to talk to me. I went up and met with Coach Brown. He talked about redshirting and a couple of other things. I left there and went back to school that day. I

B. H. Born (University of Kansas Archives)

told my coach, "I don't know what they want me to do. If they want me to walk on or what." He called them and came back. And I'll never forget, he came in my math class, and said, "Yeah, they want to give you a scholarship." I said, "Well, is that a question?" I was just ecstatic.

Really, the behind-the-scenes story was that Coach Brown had met with KU's athletic director Monte Johnson's wife, Kay Johnson, who is a realtor in town. She was driving him around town, showing him houses. They got to talking. Monte Johnson's son was on my high school team. They talked about me. He saw the tape of my state championship game; I had a really good game. He offered me a scholarship, sight unseen. And he offered Mark Turgeon a scholarship, sight unseen. He also offered Cedric Hunter a scholarship, sight unseen. We were his first three recruits when he came in here that year. So I just kind of fell into it. The timing was good.

Paul Mokeski

A lot of people think the California connection started with Adonis Jordan, Chenowith, Pierce and guys like that. But way back in the 1970s, there was a really good group of players in California. And I was drawing a lot of attention. I was one of the top big guys in the country, growing up outside Los Angeles in the San Fernando Valley. I had never heard of KU or Kansas. I grew up watching UCLA play, the great teams of Lou Alcindor and Bill Walton. Every Friday night they had a tape-delay of the Thursday night game at 12 o'clock. I remember staying up and watching those games since I was a little kid. When I was getting to be a pretty good ballplayer in high school, a lot of people kind of assumed that I was going to UCLA because of the big man connection there and I grew up a UCLA fan. I kind of went against that for a couple of reasons.

I didn't want to do what people expected me to do, and the other thing is that I kind of wanted to venture out and get away from home a little bit. I took five or six visits—to NC State, Washington State, Arizona State, USC, Gonzaga and then Kansas. It was kind of funny because I'd never been on a plane before, and then all of a sudden I'm in the air every weekend going to some school. It was plush treatment, getting shown all around the schools. But I was still a kid and didn't know what was going on, kind of getting more and more confused. But, after visiting KU, it felt natural. It felt right. It felt like the place I needed to be. And the way the people treated me, not just the coaches and the guys on the team–at one point I just told the coach, "I'm going to walk around campus." I think it was in the springtime, so there wasn't any snow and that didn't throw me off. I just kind of walked around campus and people were very friendly and said "Hi, how are you doing?" Really, in the Los Angeles area, it's not like that at all. I loved the campus, loved the tradition, loved the fieldhouse. Back then the Jayhawk Towers were new, so that was pretty neat. It just felt right, and I really enjoyed the coaching staff. Duncan Reid is the guy who recruited me. He's from Illinois, and he's the one who brought Norm Cook to KU along with other recruits. And back then there weren't as many NCAA rules on recruiting. Now, I think, you can only be out for three weeks in July. Couple weeks here and there. Well, shoot, those guys were out all the time as much as they could be. And Duncan Reid, literally, lived at the Holiday Inn in the San Fernando Valley for a month. And he was either talking on the phone or at my house almost every day. And I'd tell people I just wanted him to quit bugging me so I signed the papers to come to KU. Actually, it just felt right.

Dave Robisch

I'm sure my Dad didn't tell me about all the phone calls we got. We started with the process of narrowing it down, as quickly as we could, to five schools that I thought I would want to attend. Dad filled me in on what was going on, and we tried to come up with a reasonable number. In those days, you signed in the spring. Coach Miranda got me interested in KU, and one of the things that was special was that they stayed in touch with me on a regular basis. I just kind of hit it off with Coach Miranda, and KU was at the top of the list from the beginning. I can remember Coach Owens coming to the house in the spring of my senior year, and he was still thinking that we were looking to maybe go somewhere else. He was still talking about the university and the reasons why I should attend Kansas. My Dad and I stepped out of the room for a minute, and I said, "Dad, I'm ready. I've listened to enough people and I think that I want to go to KU." So we went back into the room and told Coach Owens that I wanted to go to Kansas. He was shocked, and his mouth went open and he said, "Did I hear what you just said?" Because he hadn't even given me all his special stuff yet. That was special, to have the opportunity to tell Coach Owens that I wanted to come to KU when he really wasn't expecting it yet. The whole recruiting process was interesting. My Dad controlled most of it, but obviously I had the final say in what schools I was really interested in.

Sam Miranda
(Assistant Coach, 1964-76)

A native of Collinsville, Illinois, Sam Miranda was a top player for the Indiana Hoosiers in the early 1950s. He joined Ted Owens's coaching staff in 1964 as the top varsity assistant coach and was also in charge of the Jayhawks' recruiting program. Miranda's top recruits included Jo Jo White, Dave Robisch, Tom Kivisto and Rick Suttle.

Everybody in the country was after Robisch. Dave was six foot ten, and he had broken all the Illinois state tournament scoring records—just an outstanding player and good student. We had him out in the fall for a football game, and the visit went well and everything. We went back a few times to see him play, that type of thing. It kind of came down to Arizona State, Kansas, Illinois, and possibly Michigan. Ted [Owens] and I went to Dave's house right after the state tournament had finished. This was probably a month before anybody could sign. Anyway, we go in there to see him and we're talking, just making sure that we can stay in the picture and everything. Dave's dad, Ted, myself and Dave are sitting there talking, and his dad says, "Dave, let's go out on the back porch and talk a minute. Coaches, we'll be right back in." They were out there maybe five minutes. When they came back in, his dad says, "Well, we've made a decision; he's going to come to Kansas." And that floored us. We were just trying to hold on, stay in the picture, and now we got a month of waiting time before we can sign him. Of course, everybody else still tried to go back in and get him, but that's how we got him. And of course, he turned out to be a great, great player for us.

Tony Guy

I used to go to the University of Pittsburgh basketball camp every year because that's where my high school coach would work. It was kind of a neat thing. At that time, Pitt had an assistant coach by the name of Bob Hill, and Bob Hill and I became real good friends. This was before I really became a good basketball player. But once I started to improve, I would hear from Bob Hill more and more. My junior year was when I started hearing from every school in the country. That was also when Bob Hill left the University of Pittsburgh and went to KU to become one of Coach Owens's assistants. At that point in time, I had already pretty much determined that I was going to go to Pitt or Marquette. I went to a Jesuit high school, so I really felt comfortable in that environment, in that structure. That's why I was looking at Marquette. And I really wanted to play for Al McGuire. The only problem was Al McGuire retired my senior year. Then Coach Hill called.

"Tony, do me a favor, would you at least just come out and look at Kansas?" I said, "Yes, Coach, that's the least I can do." So I came out to Lawrence, and I fell in love with the campus. I came to the University of Kansas based on my love for the campus. I grew up in the inner city, the concrete jungle. I saw the rolling hills, big trees, green grass, and it was really a no-brainer for me. So that's why I came to the University of Kansas. I didn't know much about the basketball program, didn't know about the players, coaches, anything like that. I just came based on my love for the campus.

Kevin Pritchard

Coach Brown is an unbelievable bench coach, but I don't think recruiting was one of his greatest strengths. He came down to watch me a couple times, but it actually started when I was a sophomore and went to the KU basketball camp. He saw me there, and then what they did was at night, we would just all scrimmage–the best players and some of the college players were there. I was playing against some of the guys who were on the current team when I was a sophomore in high school. I remember I made a move, made a layup and got fouled, and Coach Brown just went off on me. He was just yelling at me because I didn't pass the ball first. That was my first experience with Coach Brown. After my sophomore year, I thought, "Boy, I'll tell

Kevin Pritchard (Lawrence Journal-World)

you what, I don't know if that's who I want to play for, and I don't know if that's the right situation for me." Obviously three years later I ended up signing there, because I knew he would make me the best player I could be.

Adonis Jordan (1989-93)

The first recruit to commit to Roy Williams, Jordan became one of KU's all-time best point guards. The five-foot-eleven Reseda, California, product joined the Jayhawks' starting lineup

Adonis Jordan (Lawrence Journal-World)

his sophomore year and promptly led KU to the Final Four and national championship game. Jordan was also instrumental in the Jayhawks' run to the Final Four in 1993. For his career he played in 137 games for Kansas, scored 1,373 points, made 179 three-pointers, and dished out 568 assists.

B asically, Coach Williams came out to my high school a few times when he was recruiting me and another player who went to my high school. Then I went out to Lawrence on a visit, went to "Late Night" and had a great time. It was a real family atmosphere. That's the thing that stuck out the most. All the other schools that I visited–Seton Hall, Providence, UTEP and USC–were more like a business-type deal. It came down to Kansas and Seton Hall, and actually I would have started as a freshman at Seton Hall–they promised me that. But it just felt right going to Kansas. At KU, I got the sense of the family environment and that Coach Williams was genuine.

When the announcement came out about the probation and everything, I guess I looked into it a little deeper, saw that it didn't really affect me directly. My senior year in high school they weren't allowed to play in the tournament. But once I got there, we were allowed to play in the tournament, so basically the probation was only, I think, the number of scholarships they can give out. I guess that could have affected me in a way. At that time, my main thing was playing on TV and playing in the tournament. Those two things were still there my freshman year, so I didn't really think it would affect me dramatically. I was Coach Williams's first signing.

Bud Stallworth

I was recruited as the first black player to go to the University of Alabama as well as the University of New Orleans. I didn't feel comfortable about being the first black player at the University of Alabama or Auburn because when I was being recruited there, I either met all the administrative people, all the alumni that they wanted me to be introduced to, but I didn't meet the guys on the team. That was kind of odd. I knew what was going on because both of my parents were educators. We knew about segregation, we knew about the racial issues that were in the South. When you get recruited to a school to be a part of a program, and they don't take you around the team, that should raise a flag. I started to understand that this is the way society was in the South. You were treated like a second-class citizen, you could act like a second-class citizen, you became a second-class citizen. Well, fortunately for me, my parents wouldn't allow that. We were raised that once you get an education, it can never be taken away from you. You treat people the way you want to be treated; that way it'll come back to you. And if you work hard enough, there's nothing out there to stop you. The color of your skin doesn't have anything to do with it. Sure, it probably would have been nice to be at the University of Alabama back then, but another guy that played in this All-Star game with me ended up going to Auburn as their first black player, and the coach that recruited me was really angry that I didn't come there. Five years after that, he called me up. I was out here doing one of Ted Owen's camps. I was playing in the NBA. The coach said, "You really made a good decision, because the young man that came down here just committed suicide. A lot of it had to do with the way he was treated after he came to school here at Auburn."

Mike Maddox

I was recruited by Larry Brown out of Oklahoma City, and KU was one of ten schools that I looked at. In the end, it came down to Kansas and Arizona, and being from the Midwest, I just felt more comfortable at KU. And it was in the Big Eight. They had a good group of players and people that made me feel comfortable, so that's kind of how I ended up at KU.

Clyde Lovellette

I've always told the story, or made the comment, that the Kansas people were the biggest reason I came to KU because there wasn't any deviation between the Indiana people and Kansas people. I believe that both states are really down-to-earth people. To me there wasn't any phoniness. They weren't trying to butter me up. They were there to just show you what they had, and "Hey, here we are. Look at us. And you make the decision." No pressure or anything, and that, I think, is what I enjoyed the most.

B. H. Born

I was going to play pro ball, and to get ready I went back to the Shawanga Lodge in the Catskill Mountains. It was a big-time summer league, and I was going to play there all summer to get in shape. I had a contract with Ft. Wayne in the NBA, which turned out to be Detroit. I ran into this high school kid back there–Wilt Chamberlain–and he was being coached by a fellow named Red Auerbach. When we were getting ready to play them, Auerbach said to Chamberlain, "Now this fellow, Born, was an All-American in college, Wilt, so just do your best. He'll probably chew you up, but you just go ahead and do the best you can." He chewed me up. This was in 1954-55, when he was going into his senior year in high school and I had just finished my senior year in college. Afterward, Wilt and I sat together on the hill and talked. He asked me about Kansas and what it was like. I told him it was a good school and a good place to go. I called Dr. Allen and told him that this high school kid I played against was the best I'd ever seen. He ended up going to KU, of course, and he was also

Bob Billings (*University of Kansas Archives*)

a quarter-mile champion there, and then he took second in the conference in the high jump.

Bob Billings

When I was in high school out at Russell, Kansas, I happened to enjoy some success in both basketball and football. I wasn't recruited by the world, but I had opportunities to go to a number of places. One of which was to play football at Oklahoma. The other was to come and play basketball at KU. When Dr. Allen called me in the summer of 1955, he said that Wilt Chamberlain was coming to KU and that he might go out for basketball. He thought it would be good if I could come and join them. So that's kind of the way it worked. I already had a brother at KU, so my leanings would have been to KU even though an awful lot of my Russell friends were K-State people. Obviously I had a chance to go to K-State to play either football or basketball or both back then. Today, I would have been a very strong candidate for at least the A-team in a fraternity.

I always like to say that if it hadn't been for Wilt coming here, I might have ended up trying to play football at Oklahoma. But I always said that because I wanted Wilt to feel really good about our relationship. And it was a wonderful decision because the University of Kansas in Lawrence, obviously, has been my life for the last 45 years or so. I was very lucky to have the opportunity.

Jeff Boschee (1998-2002)

The Valley City, North Dakota, native finished an outstanding career at KU in 2002. Boschee earned All-Big 12 Conference Honorable Mention for the second time following his senior season. The six-foot-one guard also set the Kansas record for most three-pointers in a career, finishing with 338. The Big 12's Freshman of the Year in 1999, Boschee also captured the Most Outstanding Player award at that year's conference tournament. He averaged 13.4 points per game in 2002 and was a major contributor to KU's run to the Final Four. Boschee played in 137 games for KU, scored 1,560 points, and dished out 425 assists.

I narrowed my choices down to Arizona, Minnesota and Kansas. I committed to Kansas early, in the middle of August, since that was really where I wanted to play. I watched the Kansas Jayhawks when I was growing up. The opportunity came, so I didn't want to pass it up. I came on an official visit for "Late Night" with Coach Williams.

Coming to KU was what I thought it would be, a well-run program, classy, nothing under the table or anything like that. The program looks just the way it is on TV. And I always watched Coach Williams growing up. He always had class, and the way he ran his program was the right way. It was everything I thought it would be.

Roger Morningstar

I was real lucky, is kind of what happened. I was a kid who developed later, grew later, whatever you want to call it. My freshman year at a little junior college in southern Illinois, I grew about four inches. We had a real good team, but no really good players. We played in the state championship, and Sam Miranda, who was the assistant at KU, was actually at that game to watch another player on the other team. It was one of those deals where I just had a pretty good game and he saw something he liked. And then the next year, the same group of kids—we were all freshmen—we won that regional tournament and went to Hutchinson for the national tournament, and that was just kind of how it transpired. There was a lot of being in the right place at the right time. I've always been big on tradition and history and knew very well who had played at KU and what kind of program it was. It was really a no-brainer decision for me.

Another reason. I remember my freshman year, on a Saturday afternoon, watching Kansas play Notre Dame on TV and thinking, "Wow, these are two awfully good programs." But both teams were not very good that year. I can remember very well the fact that I thought, "Gee, there's two really good teams that are struggling a little bit, they might need some help. And there might be an opportunity to play at either place." And that had a lot to do with the decision. The fact that there was a kid at KU named Tom Kivisto, who is from the same general area, the Chicago area, that I was from, helped. Tom was the best high school player I ever saw. Although we didn't know each other personally, we had played against each other. He was a year ahead of me, and he was in a class all by himself. He was just tremendous. I was in awe of Tom, and the chance of playing with him and trying to get Kansas turned around was a great challenge, and something that I very much looked forward to.

Sam Miranda

When we recruited Jo Jo White out of St. Louis, I had just gotten to KU. I called up a fellow I knew that coached in St. Louis and asked him who the better basketball players in the St. Louis area were. He said, "Well, Sam, the best player by far is Jo Jo White. If you can get him, you don't even have to see him play. Just take him." Jo Jo was a midyear graduate. That's what they had back in the bigger cities in those days. I went back to see him and called him all the time. The first time I went back I talked to his dad and mother. His dad said, "Well, Coach, this is kind of new to us. We've not been through this very much at all in regard to college recruiting. We'd like Jo Jo's high school basketball coach to have a big say in this." So naturally, I started to visit with Jo Jo's coach quite a bit. We were out to lunch one day in St. Louis, and I was going over all the things that I thought would be great for Jo Jo if he came

Jo Jo White (University of Kansas Archives)

to KU, and at the end of that, the coach said, "Jo Jo, that sounds good to me." And that was it. Jo Jo came out to visit, went to the football game during which Gayle Sayers ran the opening kickoff back for a touchdown against Oklahoma. KU won at the end on a two-point play, 15-14, and the crowd ran out on the field. He kind of liked that. We did a good job of recruiting Jo Jo and everything, but his high school coach saying to him, "That sounds good to me, Jo Jo," I think that's what did it for us.

In recruiting, I've always felt there's one person in the family–it could be dad, mom, an uncle, brother, whoever–someone is going to have the number-one say besides the boy about where to go to school. So if you can zero out who you think the key person is in that recruiting process–not that you're going to ignore the other people–you're really going to spend a lot of time with that one person who could be instrumental in helping you recruit the prospect.

John Parker

How did I end up at the University of Kansas? Well, originally, I looked all around. I had a chance to go about any place I wanted to go. I was an All-State quarterback in high school, but I'd been hurt several times, so I decided I wanted to play basketball. I wrote a letter to KU and I told them I'd like to play basketball, who I was and everything. KU decided they wanted to give me a full scholarship, but they also wanted me to throw the javelin. I'd won the state championship my junior and senior year throwing the javelin, so I said sure. It didn't take much to do that, just go out and throw the javelin at track meets, and they decided to give me a scholarship.

CHAPTER 5

Home Court Advantage

The advantage KU has when they play at Allen Fieldhouse can be overwhelming for visiting teams. Considering the Jayhawks' first home courts–the basement of Snow Hall, a skating rink and the local YMCA–a home court advantage wasn't as important as having a permanent playing site in the early years of Kansas basketball. When Robinson Gymnasium opened in 1907, the Jayhawks finally had a real court.

Kansas began playing in Hoch Auditorium in 1927, and it served the team well. The need for more seats–a lot more–led to the construction of Allen Fieldhouse, which was dedicated on March 1, 1955. Named for Coach Phog Allen, the Jayhawks started things off right in their new home by defeating K-State, 77-67, in the inaugural game.

"In this hour of great recognition of my services to the University of Kansas," Allen said when he found out the new fieldhouse would be named for him, "I feel very unworthy and deeply grateful."

The Jayhawks take the floor during their first-ever practice at Allen Fieldhouse in 1955. (University of Kansas Archives)

John Parker

Hoch Auditorium was a theater with a basketball floor in front, and it was a terrible place to play. It was a joke for a college. When we moved into Allen Fieldhouse, it was the difference between night and day. At that time, I believe it was the best and largest fieldhouse in the United States.

People didn't want to see us; they wanted to see Wilt. Of course, they wanted to see us all, too, because we were good, but Wilt was the drawing card. Every place we went, we played in front of a sellout crowd. At that time, they apparently didn't have a fire marshal in Lawrence–they had people standing everywhere. At one end of the floor at Allen

Action at Hoch Auditorium in the 1930s. (University of Kansas Archives)

Fieldhouse, people crowded up as close as they could for most of our home games.

Otto Schnellbacher

Hoch Auditorium was a great place to play because it had some quirks to it. Behind one basket, the wall slanted. It was closer to the court on one side than the other side. If you didn't know that, you could really bang into that wall. If you're going in toward the seats, the wall ran away from the floor. Going in toward the stage, the wall ran toward the court. You had to be careful going in from the right-hand side. But it was a fun place to play in.

Charlie Hoag

I remember Hoch Auditorium had a wood floor laid on concrete. We didn't practice on it that much because you'd get shin splints–the floor just didn't give. The way the floor was laid out, there were funny angles and a stage on one side, theater seats on the other. But it was also a place that was very, very good to the home team because of the way the baskets were hung, the angles behind the baskets, and stuff like that. I can remember having to actually stand between people's legs to throw a ball in from out of bounds. Of course, there was a lot of that back in those old arenas.

Clyde Lovellette

Coming from the high school gyms I played in, Hoch was, other than the bleachers on both sides, a pretty big place as far as I was concerned. It was different, but Hoch was a big thing for me. It was a great atmosphere for basketball. It's too bad all the students couldn't get in for each game. They had to split the student body into different groups–names ending with A, B, C through F would get tickets for one game, and F through something else another game. It was a shame we didn't have Allen Fieldhouse when we played. I think we could have filled it just like the boys do now.

B. H. Born

I didn't have any problems running at Hoch, but the floor was hard. We used to have problems with those flags flying behind the goals. They put these black flags up

In addition to the quirky wall angles and stage at Hoch Auditorium, the floor was very hard with little or no give. (University of Kansas Archives)

so you'd get a little better perspective on the goal. The visiting teams always raised hell because of those black flags flying—they thought it was like a pirate ship.

Dave Robisch

Allen Fieldhouse is a special place. Obviously, the tradition is so special. You look at the players that played there before I did, and the players that have played there since, and I think that you can feel the tradition when you step onto the court with the band playing and the cheerleaders and the pom pom squad. And the fans are so extraordinary. Then you walk outside the floor and you see the history of championships and other players that have played there with The Wall of Fame and the Hall of Fame.

Allen Fieldhouse, to me, is one of the best five places to watch a basketball game. I may be prejudiced because I went there, but to me, there's no doubt. You can talk about North Carolina. You talk about Duke, now, and Kentucky. There are only so many special programs, to me, in the country, and Kansas certainly deserves the right to be in that situation with Allen Fieldhouse. To me, there's no finer place in America. And if you listen to other people, sportscasters or news writers or people that have come in and watched a game there, they know. They see how special it is.

Paul Mokeski

What really stands out in my four years at KU is the atmosphere of Allen Fieldhouse. I remember my first week in Lawrence was followed by a long weekend. Everyone went home except me. I was really the only guy who lived that far away. The Jayhawk Towers, where the athletes lived, were pretty empty. I remember walking from the Towers and sitting in the empty fieldhouse and just kind of daydreaming about hearing my name announced, seeing it on the scoreboard, and then having that really happen. I remember the walks from Jayhawk Towers to the fieldhouse before a big game, against Kansas State or Missouri, and walking by all the people that slept out in the tents or waiting there and coming out for warmups way before the game. I don't think there's anything you can duplicate or explain to anybody about running out of that tunnel into the fieldhouse when it's packed and that rush you get knowing you're a Jayhawk. Dallas was a loud place to play in, and Sacramento is one of the loudest places to play. A reporter asked me once, "Is that the loudest you ever heard?" I said, "No, two places were louder–the Boston Garden and Allen Fieldhouse."

Tony Guy

My freshman year, we played against the Soviet team in our first game at home. The team started running out of the tunnel, and I'm kind of at the back end of the line. All of a sudden Allen Fieldhouse erupts, and I start getting chills. I almost turned around and went back into the locker room, because no one had prepared me for that. I thought, "Oh, no. I can't play here." There were too many people in the place, and I almost vomited, that's how scared I was. No one talked about that. No one prepared you for that experience, the first time you run out that tunnel. I thought that was awesome, and it scared me to death. Obviously, I got used to it. But no one can prepare you for the first time you run out on that floor for your first game.

Jeff Boschee

Since my freshman year, every time I'd run out of that tunnel at Allen Fieldhouse and hear those 16,000 people scream, it gave me goose bumps up and down my spine. It's almost like everyone sits right on top of you in a little, tight area, and they get so loud in there. I remember some of the Missouri games–especially the Missouri game this year [2002]–were just jam-packed. People standing, up at the top of the building. It's a great college basketball environment.

Greg Gurley

My best KU memory is my last game as a senior at Allen Fieldhouse in 1995, the one and only game I started in my career. We were tied with Oklahoma

A familiar sight to KU fans–a jam-packed Allen Fieldhouse. (University of Kansas Archives)

State for the Big Eight regular season championship, and whoever won that game would win the conference. I started, had 13, 15 points, a really good game for me. I got knocked out in the first half–concussion–the whole deal. I went in the locker room, got all juiced up, whatever. They banged my head around, made sure I was okay, and I came back out and had a good second half. So for me, personally, that was my greatest memory. We won the game and won the league championship.

Bud Stallworth

It was electric. We ran through a hoop–the players burst through one before every game–and I liked that. We'd hit that floor, and the band would break out in the fight song. It really pumped us up. There's no amount of money in the world that they can pay you to make you feel as good as you do when you run into Allen Fieldhouse as a basketball player. There's nothing like it. I played five years in the NBA and I never ran on the court feeling the way I felt running onto the Allen Fieldhouse court. In New Orleans, they even had a band leading us out onto the floor. And it wasn't the same. There is just not any place that I played–and I've been at the Finals in the NBA where the Sonics beat the Bullets, and they had a nice crowd with adrenaline flowing and everything. It still didn't feel the same. I can't compare what it was like running out on the court at Kentucky, Duke, North Carolina or UCLA, but I know how I feel when these [current KU teams] come in the house and run out there, because I know how it felt for me to do it. And they have embellished it more now, because they've got better sound equipment and light shows and all that. And when they pump up the music and you come out the tunnel and onto the court, pop through that piece of paper they've got and jump out there with the crowd humming, there's nothing like it, a feeling you'll have for the rest of your life.

Roger Morningstar

I get chills when I think about it. [Everyone] on earth should be able to play at a place like Kansas. Everything was just right for me: the tradition, the beautiful campus, everything that you think of. Some kids go to school just to play basketball and some kids go to school just for an education. I love tradition, and I love history, and I love being part of something that has great tradition and history. I love a beautiful campus. I've seen a lot of schools that have good basketball teams, like UNLV, for example. But it's just a bunch of buildings on a bunch of flat ground. Nothing unique or nice about it. All that stuff played with me, and I feel so fortunate to have been able to play in a place like Allen Fieldhouse.

Paul Mokeski

I went to high school in California, and we had the only gym back then that had a tartan surface [basketball court] in all of Los Angeles. I played on tartan for four years in high school. And in the Pac-10 Conference, Washington State had a tartan floor. On the day before UCLA would go up to play Washington State, they would practice on our court, on our tartan surface. Then when I got to KU, there was that tartan surface again. It was supposed to be a multipurpose floor, to hold up better. And it was supposed to stop injuries, but really, it kind of did the opposite. It kind of got dented and torn up, and it looked grungy. Man, stopping on that floor was tough, and it was hard to get any spring. I remember–not that we didn't like to play in Allen Fieldhouse–but we liked to go to Nebraska because they had a new, wood floor. It felt like we were jumping off a trampoline on that wood floor.

I think they changed the floor at Allen the year after I left. We played on it the full four years I was there. I know they played on a raised floor before that. My legs, I can feel it now. That was the floor back then that was the newest high-tech invention. It just never turned out like it was supposed to.

Tony Guy

One neat thing about Darnell Valentine was that he was regarded as such a great player that if he

Allen Fieldhouse (University of Kansas Archives)

said something, Coach Owens would listen to him. Darnell had sprained his ankle a couple times on the tartan surface that was in Allen Fieldhouse my first two seasons at KU, and he was tired of that floor. It was a rubber surface, supposedly maintenance-free compared to a wood floor. But you could tear your knees up on it, hurt your ankles on it. It was brutal–rubber over concrete. So Darnell finally went into Coach Owens's office and complained. A couple days later, we had a new wood floor. Way to go, Darnell.

Mike Maddox

Allen Fieldhouse is as good a place as there is to play college basketball. The minute I walked in there on my recruiting trip, it smelled like a gym, it looked like a gym. It just had a great feel. The stands are terrific. When we walked out on that floor, we knew we had an advantage. It was kind of amazing to go out against some of the teams, the lesser teams—non-Big Eight teams that had never been there before. You could just see the look in their eyes that they were a little bit overwhelmed. It was just a great place for us to play.

CHAPTER 6

Return to Glory
Larry Brown

The Kansas basketball program, rich with history and tradition, had slowly slipped over a seven-year period. Between 1976 and 1983, KU made just two trips to the NCAA Tournament and won the Big Eight Conference just once. When Ted Owens was fired following the '83 season, Larry Brown–because of North Carolina coach and KU alum Dean Smith's recommendation–became the sixth head coach at the University of Kansas.

He was the right choice.

Brown quickly returned the program to national prominence, as Kansas won the Big Eight tournament his first season as coach. KU returned to the Final Four in 1986 and two years later won the national championship as Danny Manning led his teammates on a surprising run through the tournament and shocked the basketball world. The Jayhawks defeated Oklahoma, 83-79, to win Kansas's second national championship. In all, Brown led Kansas to five consecutive NCAA Tournament appearances. His overall record at KU was 135-44.

In the summer of 1988, Brown left Kansas for the San Antonio Spurs of the NBA. The basketball program, because of violations made under Brown, was placed on probation in the fall of 1988.

Chris Piper

We were playing in the Great Alaska Shootout, it would have been the 1984-85 season. We were playing Maryland, and for some reason, I was in the game. I have no idea why; I think we were in bad foul trouble and it was the last possession of the game. I got put in for defense, and I remember praying, hoping, that Len Bias wouldn't dunk on me. We ended up winning, and one of the things that I always remember about that game was coming out off the floor after we won it. It was a tight game, and Calvin Thompson was really excited. He kept saying, yelling really, "We've got the best coach, we've got the best coach." It really was true. We had a guy in Coach Brown that we might not always like playing for and practicing for because he was very demanding, but he got the best out of you. And we knew going in that we had the best shot of winning because we had the best coach on the bench. A great matchup player coach, too. He sees things on the floor and really knows how to push buttons during a game as well.

Chris Piper (Lawrence Journal-World)

Coach was an extremely smart basketball guy. It's just amazing the things he sees on the floor. You'd run a play and he could run five possessions back into the whole series and tell you exactly what you did wrong, if you were two feet out of place or whatever. Really big on coaching on the floor. He's hard to get to know. He's very quiet, but we had a good time. They were tough years, awfully tough years, because he was trying to change things around, get a new mindset there. One thing that we always knew going on the floor was that we had the best coach sitting on the bench with us.

Restoring KU's Basketball Tradition

"It means a lot to me to be a part of this program," Larry Brown said after he was hired as the Jayhawks' new head coach. "I want it to be like a North Carolina or a Louisville, like it used to be, but that can't happen overnight. There's a tradition here that is very special to me, and I want to contribute to it, to make Kansas a program people respect year in and year out."

Resolution No. 6124

Following the Jayhawks' championship run in the 1988 NCAA Tournament, the House of Representatives of the State of Kansas introduced Resolution No. 6124, "A Resolution congratulating and commending the University of Kansas men's basketball team and Coach Larry Brown for winning the NCAA National Championship for 1988."

The resolution noted the major accomplishments of the team, individual awards given to Coach Brown and Danny Manning, and Ryan Gray, the adopted "team mascot."

The resolution concluded with more congratulations and commendations and directed the Chief Clerk of the House of Representatives to send enrolled copies of the resolution to Chancellor Budig, Director of Athletics Bob Frederick, Coach Brown, the assistant coaches, team members, and of course, Ryan Gray.

Larry Brown (University of Kansas Archives)

Larry Brown (Head Coach, 1983-88)

After the Jayhawks won the 1988 NCAA Championship, Larry Brown addressed 30,000 fans celebrating at KU's Memorial Stadium.

"I've always wondered what this would be like. It was unbelievable. You get a sense of pride when you coach at Kansas because of what Phog [Allen] did and what all the other players and coaches have done, and when you are recognized like that, it's going to take a while for it to sink in."

Chris Piper

Those early years with Coach were tough because all the players he had for the most part were Ted Owens's players. Great, great talent, but they really didn't know how to play the game the way he wanted it to be played. When you watch Larry Brown in college you'd know all about the team game. It was tough. In 1985, I think we were 26 and eight. Pretty darn good, and it was a very miserable year because he expected more out of us and we didn't get there. The season was over, and we came home and it was curfew. We had curfew from there until school was out. Just trying to change the mindset of the team. It obviously did some good, because the next year we went to the Final Four and I think we lost only four games.

Coach is very demanding and very vocal. You had to have the right mentality to play for Coach. You had to be sure of yourself, have good self-confidence. Because he would tear you down and really come after you, test you. He really believed in toughness. I think that's hard sometimes until you figure out that what he's doing is really for your benefit. You can't sit there and think, "Oh, he's picking on me."

Should I Leave, Stay, or Go?

After KU won the 1988 NCAA Tournament, Larry Brown was ready to leave Lawrence and return to UCLA as the Bruins' head coach. He found it hard to leave, though, at least for a while.

"I told [UCLA] I was going to come. We were just going to work out the details and give me the opportunity to tell our athletic director and basketball team that I was going to be the coach at UCLA. When I got back to Lawrence, I started to think about the things UCLA was going to do for me, and I haven't done anything for UCLA. They were more than fair, but I just didn't feel comfortable with it. And the bottom line is I decided it would be best for everybody concerned if I stay in Lawrence and the University of Kansas.

"I'm committed to these kids; I'm staying. I don't want anything to take away from the championship. Like Dorothy said, 'There's no place like home.'"

The lure of the dollar proved too much for Brown, though, and when the NBA's San Antonio Spurs came calling with a multimillion dollar contract, Brown couldn't say no, and he was gone.

"I talked to [Larry Brown] yesterday and he didn't say he was leaving," Kansas player Milt Newton said, "but he told me what the offer was and all the benefits and how he would be in control of the team. He asked me how I would feel about that, and I told him that we felt like if you leave, you've always been doing things for other people–it was time for him to do something for his interest."

"I thought I'd be at Kansas for a long time," Brown said after the announcement was made that he was going to San Antonio.

Kevin Pritchard

Obviously, I had mixed emotions, because as a junior and senior coming up, I was going to be looked to lead the team, and know how he is toward the other players. He's hard on them, but he also gives them a lot of freedom. So I kind of had mixed emotions. But I knew that he had a great deal, going to San Antonio and being back in the NBA. That was something he wanted. I also wouldn't want my coach to be in college, or to be at Kansas, when he didn't absolutely want to be there.

Mike Maddox

Coach Brown is a tremendous basketball coach. I don't think I've been around anybody smarter when it comes down to the Xs and Os of basketball. He was a demanding coach and not always the easiest guy to play for. But he was a very, very good coach and I learned a lot about basketball from him.

I didn't have a lot of problems with him. I was only with him for a year, and I was a freshman. It was a little different. He'd get on guys, he'd get on guys hard. There were some guys who couldn't deal with it, some players who had a real hard time playing in that environment. He was a demanding guy, and there was no mystery on how he felt about what you were doing. Some guys thrived in that environment, and there were other guys who kind of struggled with it.

Chris Piper

We were at Washington, kind of early in the 1988 season, and we were down. They were bombing away on us and everything was going in. Coach Brown finally substitutes, takes me off the bench and puts me in, puts the guy on the bench that was just getting killed out there. Then he put Milt Newton in as well. And they still kept hitting shots on us. We're down by 20, we call a timeout,

Mike Maddox (Lawrence Journal-World)

and they had just hit three shots in a row. I'm thinking "Oh, my God. He's going to lose a vein on the side of his head at this timeout." And he was like, "You know what, guys? The Lakers couldn't beat these guys today if they keep hitting shots. You're playing great defense; just keep on doing what you're doing. We're going to be fine." So we put a full-court press on, start slowly whittling away, and sure enough, they start missing shots. We were playing good defense when we had that different substitution pattern on the floor. We ended up winning that game by ten points. To me, that was the turning point for us in 1988. We still had a few bad games after that, but Coach, I think, saw that game, and said, "You know what? The guys that have the most talent aren't going to play hard, and they're not going to do things, so I'm going to play the guys that will." We lost Archie Marshall a few games later at St. John's. That was a tough, tough thing. Milt came in in place of Archie, and Milt did all the right things. We finally had a team on the floor that we knew was going to play hard and play great defense. And then the season started changing for us.

Kevin Pritchard

You know Coach Brown is tough on everybody. But to a guard trying to understand a new system, he can be really, really tough. That's his strength. He kind of breaks you down and then builds you up. My freshman year, I didn't start the first four or five games, and when I became a starter, he was even tougher on me.

I think he knew that I had good potential, and he was trying to bring it out of me. I know that we played some early games against some really good teams, and I had some good games. I remember thinking after a game, "Wow, that was a really good game. I played a really good game." He was never happy with it; he was always tough on me and made sure I was always focused on the next game and getting better. His whole thing is getting better–you have to get better every day.

The Same, but Different

Dean Smith, KU alum and college basketball's all-time winningest coach, saw the differences in

Larry Brown and Roy Williams, but he also saw the similarities.

"Larry had tried to hire Roy as an assistant," Smith said of Brown. "They're very different personalities, but much about Larry and Roy are similar. They're both enthusiastic, fierce competitors, great teachers and have charisma.

"They each brought something to KU that it needed at the time."

Kevin Pritchard

Well, you know, one of the reasons I think they recruited me was because I wasn't afraid to take the big shot. I like the ball in my hands, and there'd been some games previously where Coach Brown didn't feel like I was shooting enough, especially down the stretch. I made the big shot against St. John's my freshman year. The play before I hit it, I missed a three-pointer. I was so mad at myself because I got a great look. And St. John's went into the zone, and because I missed the last shot, they were really hesitant to run out on me again, and I just grabbed it, shot it and made it. And it was all in rhythm. I remember coming over to the bench and Coach Brown was like, "I've been telling you to shoot that all season. Keep shooting it." Boy, I'll tell you what, that really meant a lot to me that he knew I was going to make it, and I had confidence in myself and he had confidence in me.

Going into the [1988] NCAA Tournament was the first time I felt really good about playing the point guard position. It was uncomfortable at the beginning just

Kevin Pritchard (Lawrence Journal-World)

because in Coach Brown's system, you're calling the offense, you're calling the defense, you're calling the out-of-bounds plays. He obviously helps you with that, but there are so many responsibilities that were completely new. I remember the very first time he tried me out at the point, and I took it down the left-hand side and I went by my guy with my left hand and shot it with my left hand and barely missed it. I was furious with myself. I was like, "Oh, my gosh, how did I miss that?" And Coach Brown was going crazy, saying "Oh, my God! What a great play." And I'm thinking, "Two weeks ago, if I was playing the shooting guard position and I missed that he would have gone crazy–in a bad way. Now I'm playing the point guard and I barely miss it, and he thought it was the greatest play, because what he was doing now, I realized, was trying to see if I could take the ball left-handed all the way. He was more excited about that than anything I'd done in the previous month. I think that really tells you a lot about him.

He sees the game at a very fine point. I personally don't think there's a coach out there who sees the game like he does. He sees it on a level that probably only a few men have ever seen it. Coach Brown looks at basketball and he's the doctor. He's the professor. He understands it better than anybody. And he can explain it better than anybody. Because of that, he makes his teams better every year. And, as a coach, that's your number-one job. Get your team better. Because you only have so much potential to work with, if you keep getting better you always know that you've got a chance.

Chris Piper

The red jerseys we wore in the 1986 Final Four–never wore those again. We wore gold jerseys one time in 1988, and then we never wore those again, either. One of the coaches, Alvin Gentry, showed up–I think it was the Final Four in 1988–with wingtip shoes on, and Coach Brown made him go back to the hotel and change because he had lost a game one time with wingtip shoes. So nobody was allowed to wear wingtip shoes any more. Yeah, Coach Brown was very superstitious.

This isn't a criticism, but one of the things that Coach does that sometimes can cause problems for him is when he thinks he can help somebody out. Some of the players we had on our team during the years I was there–the last year specifically–were guys that Coach thought he could change, thought he could help. And I understand why he does it. You just can't change some people. I thought it was a bad deal that the whole team should get tainted for something that happened that didn't even affect what was going on on the floor or any of the current players.

CHAPTER 7

Rivalries

The Jayhawks have two main rivals in basketball, Kansas State and Missouri. Through the 1980s, the Jayhawks and Wildcats played for more than state bragging rights–conference honors were usually on the line. Missouri's prowess in basketball the last two decades increased the stakes of the already bitter rivalry between the border-state schools. While many of KU's conference foes in recent years consider the Jayhawks their top rival in basketball, it is the Mizzou and K-State battles that fascinate Kansas fans, and players, the most.

Tony Guy

I will never forget when we played at K-State in the old Ahearn Fieldhouse my freshman year [1978-79 season]. As we were warming up before the game, I kept hearing this splat noise as if something was hitting the floor. I looked and saw chickens. "How cute," I thought, "they're throwing rubber chickens at us." Then I saw blood on the floor, and I couldn't imagine where it came from. Then it

Chickens invariably appeared at games in Manhattan when KU played K-State during the rivalry's glory years. This chicken watches as Jayhawk players are introduced before a game in the 1970s. (Lawrence Journal-World)

dawned on me—the K-State fans were throwing live chickens at us, and they were hitting the floor and going splat. I couldn't believe it. Nobody could ever prepare you for that type of experience as a freshman. It was a carnival atmosphere at K-State, a zoo atmosphere, and it really threw me back.

My first game in Columbia against Missouri was a similar experience–the insults that were shouted at us were so personal. It's one thing to make fun of the team, the school and that sort of thing, but when they attack you personally? They talked about your mama. They talked about your girlfriend. They had a guy walk across the basketball court in an ape uniform, and on the back it said, "I'm Wilmore Fowler's brother"–Fowler was a guard on our team. Where do you draw the line in this deal? I had never seen anything like that before in my life. So Missouri and K-State were by far the two toughest places to play.

As a basketball player, I looked forward to playing at those two places more than anywhere else, simply because they were good teams in a tough environment. I've always felt like that combination should bring out the best in you if you're an athlete.

Paul Mokeski

K-State's fieldhouse was pretty bad, but Missouri's was probably the worst with the fan group, the Antlers. They did all kinds of crazy stuff. One year we went down the day before the game. I think we were afraid of a snowstorm or something. We were staying at a hotel, and at one o'clock at night, there's this pizza guy knocking on our door, waking us up. I guess the Antlers had ordered pizza for all of us and had it delivered at one o'clock in the morning before the game. They were just crazy, period.

The Antlers did, I think, one of the most obnoxious, outrageous and bad things I saw while playing. One of the Antlers dressed up in a gorilla suit, and he had a sign around his neck that said, "Don't laugh at me, I'm Donnie Von Moore's brother." That was really bad.

Roger Morningstar

When I played, K-State was *the* game. Today, it really isn't, and I'm still shocked every time I go in Allen Fieldhouse. Playing K-State today is like they're playing Murray State or somebody. It doesn't have the same juice that it had back then. The big rivalry game has kind of shifted to Missouri, which was a big game for us, too, but not as big as K-State.

I can remember the first home game that I played against K-State. I was blown away by the people, the energy, the noise. I mean it was like nothing I had ever seen or experienced before. It was just an incredible atmosphere. And they were good; K-State was good. That was one of the reasons why I think it was such a good rivalry. Jack Hartman was there. And they had players like Lonnie Kruger and Chucky Williams and Mike Evans. Good players, but they finished second to us. The two years I played for KU, we won the Big Eight, and I believe K-State finished second both times.

Jeff Boschee

When Drew [Gooden] slammed the ball at center court at the end of the [2002] Iowa State game at Ames, that was just Drew being Drew. It wasn't a knock against the Iowa State players or Iowa State fans. Drew is a very competitive person and it was a hard-fought win. We struggled the whole game, and we finally came out on top. I think it was just kind of an exclamation point to say our work is done here. It was a tough game, and we had struggled for most of it. We got lucky when they missed some free throws, and we were able to pull it out. But Drew was just being himself.

Delvey Lewis (University of Kansas Archives)

Delvey Lewis

A highly touted recruit from Washburn Rural High School in Topeka, Kansas, Delvey Lewis was one of the Jayhawks' top backcourt performers in the 1960s. The six-foot-one guard averaged 10.9 points per game and was named to the All-Big Eight Conference team in 1966, his senior season. Lewis played in 76 games for the Jayhawks and scored 651 points.

It was pretty lively in Manhattan when we played at Ahearn Fieldhouse. The people seemed to be pretty close to the court. They had posters and other things, but the thing I remember best is when the fans, or students, threw chickens on the court. Some were painted like a Jayhawk–red and blue–some weren't.

At the Nebraska Coliseum, the people would grab your shorts, the hair on your legs, anything, when you were throwing the ball in bounds. That's how close we were to them. They literally had to part the crowd to let you throw the ball in. And they had this big marching band drum that they pounded on constantly. They even got to us on the bench, they were so close. We did get even, though. We'd hold the plastic squirt bottles, the water bottles, up to our face like we were getting a drink, but move our head and squirt the crowd behind us.

Brewer Fieldhouse at Mizzou wasn't as bad as K-State or Nebraska. The crowd wasn't as close, but the games might have been rougher. The Missouri players always took cheap shots at us.

K-State Goes Bananas

When the Kansas players were introduced before the game against K-State at Manhattan on February 11, 1978, Wildcat fans threw scores of bananas at them, the primary target being Jayhawk Donnie Von Moore. Maybe the price of poultry was too high or the imagination of the Wildcat fans too low. Whatever the reason, the banana toss at Von Moore was supposedly payback for the hot dogs hurled at K-State player Curtis Redding by KU fans the month before at Allen Fieldhouse. Redding was a bit of a "hot dog" player–the high-scoring forward from New York was known to showboat. The reason for the bananas tossed at Von Moore was presumably of an uglier tone.

"I expected it and enjoyed it," Von Moore said after the game. "It makes them look kinda dumb. They were trying to hit us and were hitting their own players."

"We seem to do well with bananas," KU's Ken Koenigs said. "They should have stayed with chickens."

K-State coach Jack Hartman (Lawrence Journal-World)

Cleaning up the mess of bananas on the court delayed the start of the nationally televised game by five minutes, something that didn't sit well with NBC. The Jayhawks didn't mind the delay and "gave the Wildcats the slip" in the game, winning 75-63.

Paul Mokeski

The KU-K-State rivalry wasn't between just the players and the coaches; both schools were emotionally involved. K-State had good basketball teams, and we were very good. I remember going into Ahern Fieldhouse at Manhattan the first time and getting introduced before the game. All of a sudden, they were throwing live and dead chickens at us. They were painted red and blue and were pooping all over the floor. Flying at us. They'd hit the floor

John Parker (University of Kansas Archives)

and the poop would fly all over the place. A couple of the chickens broke their necks when they were thrown out there. I couldn't believe it, and I remember thinking, "What the heck is going on?"

I remember before the K-State game my junior year [in 1978], we got together as a team and said, "Okay, we know they're going to throw chickens at us and all that stuff" (they actually threw bananas at us that year). So when we're introduced, instead of running out to the free-throw line, we're going to run right to the K-State bench and shake [K-State coach] Jack Hartman's hand and stand right next to him. And that's what we did. We shook Hartman's hand and stood there so they couldn't throw anything at us.

John Parker

The only place we ever had any trouble was at Missouri. Most of the people down there were not very nice to us. The only time that Maurice King–an African-American on our team–ever got in a confrontation or fight with anybody was at Missouri, and that was because of Norm Stewart. Norm was on the team then, and he was a great player. But he kept calling Maurice all kinds of names. You can imagine what, like "nigger," and so on and so forth. Maurice finally had all he could take and got in a fight. It didn't last very long, and when I say a fight, I mean he pushed him or something. Of course, the crowd went crazy, and they'd play those Southern songs like "Dixie" and all that crap. That's the only place we went that we had any trouble. We also played that year down at Rice–of course it's in the South, too–and didn't have any trouble. Missouri's actions were just a sad deal, but, of course, we won the game.

Tony Guy

One year we're playing Missouri at Columbia and Coach Owens is giving his pregame speech, and it's intense. The team was into it; everybody was thinking "We've got to beat these guys." Then Coach Owens said, "Guys, I hate Missouri. I *hate* them." And then he said, "Do you realize that Missouri was the last state to free the slaves?" We kind of looked at each other, trying to figure out where Coach Owens was going with those comments. We were just kids playing college basketball and trying to get an education. We wanted to get degrees, get out of KU, get on with our lives. And he's talking about the last state to free the slaves. That's when I realized how intense some of the coaches were, how intense our coach could be.

As a player, I did not like Norm Stewart, but I respected him a great deal, and I'll tell you why. You knew when you played against a Norm Stewart-coached team that they were going to play hard. They were going to play man-to-man

Missouri's Norm Stewart (Lawrence Journal-World)

and it was going to be tough the entire game. I really respected the way his teams played, no gimmicks, just straight man-to-man.

I also didn't like Jack Hartman. K-State had good teams and they played hard, but he made it too personal. You're talking about kids playing college basketball to get a college education. It was very obvious that Owens, Hartman and Stewart hated each other. They *hated* each other. They made it personal. But I loved playing against K-State, and I loved playing against Missouri. It didn't get any better than that.

Roger Morningstar

When we played against Nebraska, the biggest thing I remember is their coach, Joe Cipriano, who was a real character. Nebraska didn't really get much respect. They had some good teams, and he was a good coach—but he was also a real fireball. I never saw him finish a game in Allen Fieldhouse. He was thrown out for something every time. I remember, I believe it was my junior year, they had a player named Jerry Fort, a kid from Chicago who was a good player. About six foot three, skinny, really quick. He could shoot the ball. Jerry went in for a layup and Norman Cook went up and just slaughtered his shot, just hammered it. But also he knocked Jerry down—almost off the old, elevated floor. Jerry went tumbling into the cheerleaders, and the ball slammed against the backboard. It came off to somebody long and I was out on the wing and took off for a fast break. I was out ahead of everybody, and I was looking back for the ball and here it comes. I catch the ball thinking, "Hey, this is an easy layup." And I'm just about at half court when I catch the ball. I turn, take one dribble and Cipriano is out on the floor, and he grabs me. "You're not going anywhere," he said. Technical foul. He threw his coat out on the floor after that and then was thrown out of the game.

Bob Billings

Every crowd was tough because they were vociferously wanting something bad to happen to Wilt. The rest of us were just kind of tailgating with Wilt. I remember one year at Colorado, one of their players got so frustrated, he jumped up on Wilt's back and bit him on the shoulder. Right during the game. Funny things like that would happen. At Missouri, they had a guy, a kid, who would walk around on stilts while we were warming up. Then he'd go down to the Missouri end so he would be the "Stilt" for the Tigers. Fortunately, we never lost to Missouri while I was in school, and I love that.

Greg Gurley

I always looked forward to going to the Hearnes Arena at Missouri, getting dressed real quick and going out and shooting around because the Antlers were so creative. I enjoyed that. They put you in this little, tiny locker room. Most schools you go to have little, tiny locker rooms—they want to make sure you're uncomfortable.

I remember Norm Stewart yelling at the refs or Kansas players the whole game and not really coaching his team. I don't know if that's a knock on him or not, but I remember him going crazy at an official or Adonis Jordan or somebody. And that's kind of an offshoot of the Missouri fans. I think they see that and then cheer for the strangest things.

Missouri is not necessarily KU's biggest rival, but KU is definitely Missouri's biggest rival. I think it's safe to say that Missouri fans live to see Kansas fail more than they want to see their own team win. It's a great rivalry. I know some people may not believe this, but I want to see Missouri do well. I like to see the Big 12 Conference do well. When we got six teams into the NCAA Tournament, I wanted to see all six get to at least the Sweet 16, if it was possible. It was great to see two Big 12 teams get to the Final Four in 2002. Not all KU and Missouri fans feel that way, but I am definitely one of them.

I'll never forget the game at Manhattan my freshman year. I think Steve Woodberry hit a last-second shot and we won by two points After the game, Richard Scott and David Johanning kind of took on the K-State crowd by themselves. Richard was a pretty vocal guy, and he was waving at the whole K-State crowd to come and fight him. Somebody threw some pennies or rocks or something and hit Johanning in the head. He came back in the locker room, his head was bleeding and he was really mad. He wanted to go back out there and fight. It was just a funny thing because two guys versus 5,000 pissed-off K-State fans wouldn't do very well.

Coach Williams always used to tell us in the locker room, regardless of where we were, that when we're up with two minutes left to go and the fans start to leave their own gym, that is something he takes a great joy in. We did, too. He'd tell us that before a game or at the half, "Hey, let's get these fans out of here with two or three minutes to go. Let's get back to Lawrence with a victory."

My favorite place to play was probably also the toughest place for us, Gallagher Hall at Oklahoma State. It seated just 6,000 fans and was loud. And it was especially loud and packed whenever KU came to town. Usually we were ranked in the top five or top 10, and the game was on national TV. And everybody hated Kansas. We were kind of like the Yankees or Dallas Cowboys, so that brought out everyone's best. The other tough place to play was at Iowa State. I don't know what it was, but we always seemed to lose there. The Big 12 has some really tough places to play.

Tony Guy

Missouri had a really good player, Steve Stipanovich, a seven-foot All-American. He had an accident with a gun, shot himself, and then told everyone that someone broke into his room and had shot him. He missed a couple of games, and eventually the true story got out or he admitted the truth, that he shot himself. One of his first games back was against us at Allen Fieldhouse, in January, 1981. Before the game, they were announcing the starting lineups, and when they got to his name and he started to run out on the court, the fieldhouse exploded with the sound of cap guns. Sounded like a shooting range.

The poor guy. He ended up playing a terrible game. I was taken aback because as a player you go in and you're focused on the competition—what you need to do as an individual to be successful, what we need to do as a team to be successful. All of a sudden, these cap guns go off and it broke my concentration. I thought, "Oh man, they're picking on this guy." It was brutal, flat-out brutal. There's no way you could have anticipated that. And every time he touched the ball in the game, the cap guns went off again.

It was so bad, I even started feeling sorry for the guy. You're talking about a situation where I didn't like any of those guys playing for Missouri. I didn't know any of them, but I didn't like any of them, either. As an athlete, though, I really felt for Stipanovich over the abuse he was taking from our fans—of course, we ended up beating Missouri that night. And I don't know if the guy ever recovered psychologically from that incident.

Charlie Hoag

Kansas State had an excellent basketball program back then, in the early 1950s. The K-State coach, Jack Gardner, really got things going for them before Phog got back into the picture and got things going at KU again. Coach Allen was kind of pushed by Jack Gardner because of their good teams.

When the 1952 year was over, they interviewed me—season ending comments and stuff—and I made the statement that the best basketball team we played all year was K-State. And Jack Gardner wrote me a note and thanked me

Charlie Hoag (*University of Kansas Archives*)

for saying that. Of course, I said it because I meant it. I really thought they were. And that was the year we won the NCAA Tournament. They were very good and I meant it. They beat us the worst we'd been beaten all year over in Manhattan, 17 or 18 points. We turned around and beat them at home, I think by the identical difference. Phog didn't like Jack Gardner, of course, and I'm sure Jack didn't like Phog. They had a little rivalry going.

Clyde Lovellette battles hard against Missouri. (*University of Kansas Archives*)

Clyde Lovellette

K-State was always a thorn in our side. I think Phog used to say that K-State was the roughest team we played against. I felt that between K-State and Missouri, you could toss a coin over who the roughest team was. But K-State definitely had the meanest guys, especially when we played them in Manhattan. My sophomore year they intimidated us so much that I thought those guys were really out for blood. The sportsmanship went out the window with K-State. I know they're not really mean, but I was a little intimidated by them.

Paul Mokeski

I didn't know anything about KU's tradition or rivalries when I first got to Lawrence. I kind of figured out KU and K-State, but I really didn't get KU and Missouri until I got here. I think it was my freshman or sophomore year, and we were playing Missouri in Lawrence. There was a heated altercation under our basket, and I think Herb Williams–one of our players–ended up throwing a punch at one of their players. Both benches emptied, and it was pretty messy. Coach Owens and Norm Stewart were going at it at half court, really yelling at each other.

When we watched the game film the next day–the film session is where all the coaches point out what you do wrong and you never wanted them to show a play over and over again when you were at fault. We saw the altercation underneath the basket, then both benches emptying, and the whole crowd getting pushed to one corner opposite the KU bench, almost underneath the stands. Everybody was kind of involved. Some player from Missouri–he wasn't playing in the game because he had all his warmups on–goes running over there like he's going to save the day, and all of a sudden he gets enveloped by the crowd. You don't see him for a minute, and then he kind of gets spit out of the crowd. He came flying out. And he's got no warmup jacket, no sweat pants, and his jersey is all ripped. We really enjoyed watching that film. The team was cracking up, it was so funny.

Allen Fieldhouse Sabotaged

Kansas was on its way to putting a good thumping on K-State in the February 20, 1965, matchup at Allen Fieldhouse, when one of the most original and cre-

University officials prepare to remove the banners that were dropped over the scoreboard by a Wildcat fan at Allen Fieldhouse during the 1965 game with K-State.
(Lawrence Journal-World)

ative pranks was pulled in the history of the rivalry. With 8:33 remaining in the first half and KU ahead 23-9, two giant banners were unfurled–while the game was going on–over two sides of the scoreboard. They read "Go Cats. Kill Snob Hill Again." There was also a drawing at the bottom representing a broken peace pact between the two schools.

"When it fell down over the scoreboard, the thing I remember thinking more than anything else was 'How did they get it up there?'" Kansas Guard Delvey Lewis said of the banners. "That was pretty clever, but it didn't really bother us."

The K-State rooter responsible was later identified as "Wildcatman." He had hidden in a Fieldhouse closet the night before the game, positioned the banners and rigged an electrical device that dropped them during the game. The banners were removed from the scoreboard at halftime. KU won the game, 86-66.

Chris Piper

We could never beat Iowa State at Ames. Coach Brown never won there, and I don't know why. It was a tough place—they had the band playing the "Here's Johnny" song for Johnny Orr, their coach, and that would get them fired up. The unbelievable thing about Iowa State back then was that they would beat us in Ames—usually in a close game—and then they'd come into Allen Fieldhouse and we'd beat them by 30 points. They got so much adrenaline out of that crowd, and when their full-court press was working, they could always handle us. For some reason, we couldn't beat their press, and we could never win there.

Dave Robisch

When I was a sophomore, we went into Manhattan and beat K-State. There was a sign up that read, "Who's Robisch?" or something like that. The K-State fans would get on you pretty good, but it never bothered me that the crowd, the students were into it.

The biggest thing that happened with me concerning K-State carried over into the baseball season. We went to

Manhattan to play them and I was pitching the first game of a doubleheader. The stadium was packed, and the K-State fans had all come out to harass me. I pitched really well, but we lost the game, I think, 2-0. Afterwards, their fans left. The Robisch harassment was over, so they left. I always hated to lose to K-State.

We lost to them at Allen Fieldhouse my sophomore year, and that cost us the Big Eight championship or at least a tie at that point with Colorado. Those games were always special, but of course the one I remember the most was the one we lost.

Two other places were difficult for us to play in. Brewer Fieldhouse at Missouri only sat 5,000-6,000 people, the lighting was horrible and the fans were right on top of you. Obviously, they hated Kansas. It was a tough place to play and the scores were always low because of the way Coach Stewart played in those days. It was a knock-down drag-out. Finally, our senior year, we beat them in Columbia. When I'm in a game, I don't worry about what people are saying. But I do remember that that was a tough atmosphere. Colorado was about the same type of setting as Missouri, and it was just a horrible place to play. Small gym and bad lighting. We always had a tough time winning at Colorado, too.

Sam Miranda

No question, Ahearn Fieldhouse at K-State was the toughest place for us to play. It was tremendously loud, an older facility, kind of like Allen Fieldhouse, but it wasn't quite as big or nice. But the noise there was unbelievable, the crowd reactions great. When KU played there, they were really wild. Oklahoma was somewhat tough; they had a small arena that sometimes caused us problems. And Nebraska. That old coliseum–that's what they called it–was so tight on the sidelines, and they beat on that drum. That was a tough place to play.

Still, far and away, K-State was the toughest place to play. Not only a tough atmosphere because of crowd reaction, but they had a lot of talent. Tex Winter was the coach there when I first got to KU, and then Cotton Fitzsimmons came in. Outstanding coaches and good players.

Bud Stallworth

When I scored 50 points against Missouri my senior year, it was all Norm Stewart's doing. Norm had come out the day of the game and said "Bud Stallworth is having a good year, but they're not winning and my player should be player of the year." Somebody gave me that article, and I said to Aubrey Nash, our point guard and my roommate, "We're going to go out here and we're going to do some work. We aren't losing this sucker today." And Aubrey said, "You get open, and I'm going to give it to you." I said, "That's all I need. Get me the ball, because *we're not losing this game today.*"

It was the last game of my college career in Allen Fieldhouse. I had had a good relationship with the fans, and I told the guys before the game, "They're packing the house for us, even though we've had a bad year. Why don't we all sign this Frisbee–the big thing back then was throwing Frisbees–and when they introduce me, I'm going to throw it up into the stands." They introduce me and I run out there and throw the Frisbee up in the stands. About five or six years ago, I was at a football game at Memorial Stadium, and a lady came up to me and said, "You remember that Frisbee you threw in the stands at your last game?" I said, "Yeah." She smiled and said, "I got it in the divorce."

It was kind of a surreal day. My mom was there to watch me, but I wasn't feeling that well. When the game started, Norm Stewart had devised a strategy to guard me with a little guard, so I just went out of the blocks and figured I'd shoot over him all day. So that didn't work for them. Then Norm switched to a big, strong guy to cover me, but he was a little slow. So I had to take him off the block a little bit and shake him up. When that didn't work, Norm went to the box and one. And that didn't work, either.

Near the end of the game, I'm sitting on the bench—we had the game wrapped up—and somebody calls down and tells Coach Owens that I have a chance to break the Big Eight single-game scoring record, that I have 48 points. I didn't realize that I had that many points. Coach Owens put me back in the game and I was fouled. So I go to the line, make those two shots. After the game, everybody's telling me "You just broke the Big Eight scoring record." And I'm going, "Yeah. Big Eight scoring record."

"You scored 50 points." And I go, "Gee, 50 points, all of this and I'm not even tired. I could go out and play again." The fans rushed on the court, and the next I know they were carrying me off the floor.

Now if you look at the picture of the fans carrying me after the game's over, doesn't it look like we just won the national championship? The feeling was like, "This is it." All of my teammates were just going mad. The 1952 team that won the national championship was there for a 20-year anniversary celebration. KU great Clyde Lovellette came into the locker room, and I had never met him before but I had read about his accomplishments at Kansas. He said, "I've never seen anybody shoot like that." I said, "Thank you."

Funny thing, I didn't realize the game was on TV. We weren't on TV very much my whole college career. The Final Four, the regionals in Wichita, and maybe a couple of

Bud Stallworth is carried off the court after scoring a conference-record 50 points against Missouri in his final game at Allen Fieldhouse. (Lawrence Journal-World)

games going out of conference. I didn't know that one was on until after the game when a guy came up to me and said, "You don't know what you did for this town on Saturday." I asked, "What do you mean?" He said, "These bars in town were turning their lights on, blinking their Budweiser signs. Going crazy watching you score 50." And I said, "It was on TV?"

CHAPTER 8

Loyalty and Greatness
Roy Williams

The North Carolina protégé of Dean Smith, Roy Williams accepted the head coaching position at Kansas after others had turned it down, and lucky for KU he did. Williams's accomplishments–number of wins, conference titles, NCAA appearances, Final Fours, and All-American players–increase every season. As a coach, and more importantly a man, Coach Williams is about so much more than the accumulation of numbers and awards. He is about coaching, but more importantly, life in general. If ever there was an ideal basketball coach for the University of Kansas, it is Roy Williams, the Carolina native who came home to Kansas.

Greg Gurley (right) listens to his coach, Roy Williams.
(University of Kansas Archives)

Greg Gurley

As a coach and a person, Coach Williams is the whole package. I'm still around the program a lot, and I do some broadcasting, so I see him a lot. We play golf every once in a while in the summer. Last year, Scot Pollard and I had a little game against Coach and Jacque [Vaughn]. It was fun just to go out there on a personal level and have a good time. I don't know many–I may be wrong–but I don't think there's a whole lot of coaches across the country who do that on a regular basis with their guys. I think the true example of the kind of guy he is is the fact that Pollard, Vaughn and others have houses in Lawrence. There are so many guys still living in Lawrence, whether they play in the NBA or not, who are still close to the program.

Obviously his coaching ability is unparalleled. I don't need to talk about that, because if you don't know how great a coach he is, you don't know basketball. A lot of guys don't have the parents I had, and so they used Coach Williams as a father figure. You hear that a lot across the country, different guys say that about several coaches. Sometimes it's not necessarily true because I think a true father figure is with you through thick and thin. I think a lot of coaches across the country ask "What have you done for me lately?"

Basketball players graduate at Kansas; I graduated. A lot did, but there are some that didn't. It's a big deal. For every great player at KU like Paul Pierce, there are about ten Greg Gurleys who aren't going to play in the NBA. That's not a knock on anyone, it's reality, and Coach Williams helps you realize that. He doesn't ever put you down, but says, "Now, Greg, you're probably not going to play in the NBA." Hopefully I was smart enough to accept that. He really prepared you for everything. You can talk about what a great coach he is and that kind of gets old. I think the more important thing is the fact that he sticks with you no matter what. He helps guys get jobs. He helps guys get business. He helps guys get a lot of things. He's a very powerful man, and it would be very easy for him to look at Greg Gurley and say, "Hey, your days are done. Thanks for playing, I've got these new guys coming in." But he doesn't. It's a relationship I'll enjoy the rest of my life.

Nick Bradford (1996-2000)

A versatile, quick, tough performer, Bradford played guard, small forward and power forward for the Jayhawks during his four-year stint. The six-foot-seven Fayetteville, Arkansas, prod-

uct was KU's emotional team leader his junior and senior seasons and won the 1999 Clyde Lovellette Most Improved Player Award. Bradford played in 140 games, scored 806 points, and recorded 502 rebounds.

He's a great coach and just a great person who does a lot of things for a lot of people. That goes without saying. Coach Williams stays in contact with everybody that comes through here, and that's a tribute to him.

I'll finish school in my sixth year, and he paid for my last semester to make sure I finished. Not too many people know that, or realize the stuff like that that he does. It's probably one of the biggest things for me, concerning Coach Williams, of all the things he's done for me.

Shorter is Better

Coach Williams shortened the team's practice sessions during the 2002 season, and it appeared to have a positive effect on the Jayhawks.

"I think it did help this team and I've tried to give Nick Collison some credit for it," Williams said at a press conference during the '02 NCAA Tournament. "He says it was my idea because I asked him what he thought about it instead of him bringing it up first. I asked him 'What would you think about shorter practices?' and then he told me about how he had felt his first couple of years. I think the kids responded very well to shortening it down; I think I threw one player out of practice the whole year. I never threw the whole team out and then brought them back in at night, and I've done that before. I think through the entire course of the season I left practice only one time really mad where

Roy Williams (Lawrence Journal-World)

you just go in and slam the locker and leave–don't even talk to the assistant coaches and go home. They adapted to that and believed that I would stick with it as long as they gave me the effort. That really made it a lot of fun right there.

"We've had some teams where it's been a battle every day just to get them to practice. Some teams you have to push a lot harder and pull; this team I didn't . . .That in itself made me enjoy the journey even more. When push came to shove during the big moments, they played their tails off."

He Was Ready

Dean Smith knew Roy Williams was ready to step into a head coaching position, and he didn't hesitate to recommend his assistant for the KU head coaching spot.

"I've groomed all my assistants to be ready," Smith told the *Jayhawk Report* in 1990. "I feel so comfortable that any of them could take over our program in case I ever got sick. They might be unknown to the outside, but people within basketball know who they are and how they work in our system. My coaches have a lot of responsibility.

"Roy's a lot like the people of Lawrence and the Kansas area–down to earth. I just hope Kansas people appreciate him for more than wins and losses."

Mike Maddox

It's never a comfortable situation to have the coach who recruited you leave, and that change is always difficult. And honestly, the players were not all that involved in the process. When we found out that Coach Williams was coming in, we knew he had a great reputation. I had talked with several other coaches that I knew, including Eddie Fogler down at Wichita State, and they had nothing but great things to say about Roy Williams. So we were all pretty confident that things would work out.

That first year with him, it was tough. We went on probation. From the beginning, we knew we weren't going to be able to participate in the postseason. We also had a low number of players, and there were times we didn't even have ten guys to practice–we had only nine players for practice a lot. We had a new system to learn, a new style. And Coach Williams just killed us. He worked us about as hard as I've ever worked, but that ultimately set up what we were able to do the next two years.

Roy Stays Put

With the utterance of two simple words, Roy Williams gave Jayhawks fans everywhere reason to smile and celebrate.

"I'm staying."

Before more than 16,000 fans at KU's Memorial Stadium and a national television audience, Williams simplistically stated his intention of turning down North Carolina's head coaching job offer and staying at the University of Kansas, probably forever. The North Carolina media had already reported Williams accepting the Tar Heel job, but that wasn't true. And after a long week of inner retrospection and personal turmoil over what to do, Williams decided to stay put at Kansas.

"There's no question that at one point I was leaning strongly toward going," Williams said at the July 7, 2000, press conference. "When it first happened, if someone had held a gun to my head, I would have gone. It's a place I dreamed of playing at when I was a kid and dreamed of coaching at.

"But during those six days, the indecision brought up so many positives for staying at Kansas. I couldn't come to grips with leaving. It's not like I had been there two or three years. There were things I became attached to."

The decision came down to what former North Carolina head coaches Dean Smith and Bill Guthridge had taught Williams.

"After 12 years my fingerprints are on [Kansas]," Williams said. "Coach Smith did convince me that it would have been my program. But I did what he taught me to do and that's to be loyal. I tried to say that and I meant it.

"It boiled down to chasing my dream and doing what I thought was right with my players. I felt like I would have been disloyal to them. It sounds corny but that's the way Roy Williams is.

"I've said the grass is greener where I'm standing. There is a lot of movement in coaching, but that doesn't mean it's best for everybody. What was best for Roy Williams was to stay put."

Greg Gurley

Just to be honest, I think I was surprised a little bit that he stayed at KU instead of going to North Carolina. He really put the shoe on the other foot. I'm sure growing up in North Carolina, coaching there, his dream job was the head coaching position at the University of North Carolina. It had to have been the toughest decision. We were with him a lot during that week, and I think he changed his mind several times. I think ultimately he made the right decision, because that North Carolina job is great, don't get me wrong. But we're talking about 12 to 13 years since he was last there, and there's probably a different chancellor now. I know there's a new athletic director. So things change. You don't necessarily know what you're getting into. He had one of the greatest mentors ever in Dean Smith, and he could tell him what to expect. Looking at that North Carolina job, he'd have his pick of players across the country. He had to look at that. There's no way he could just say no. That's *the* job. And it was surprising to me that so many guys turned it down because that's got to be the second best job in the country. I think Kansas is the best.

There was a well-publicized comment that I made, and this was back before UNC coach Bill Guthridge retired, but there was talk about him leaving. We were at basketball camp, Rex Walters was there, Scot Pollard was there, and my wife was pregnant at the time. We were talking about just hanging out in Lawrence, enjoying the family atmosphere, and I made a comment to Coach Williams that was something like, "How many grandkids do you have now?" And he kind of looked at me and we tried to figure it out. It was no big deal. Later on, he made a statement saying that he'd thought about that during the week. "Hey, look. I do have a lot of kids. I do have a lot of grandkids, if you want to call them that." Not that that is the reason he stayed. I had reporters calling me and asking what I said to him. I was out of town at the time and I had about 50 messages from different reporters. They didn't reference the grandkids quote, and I thought to myself, "Did I say something stupid and it got taken out of context?" I was driving back home from the Ozarks, thinking, "God, I hope I didn't ..." I couldn't remember, but luckily it was that comment and it worked out great. I'm glad he stayed; everyone's glad he stayed. Obviously, I think he'll be here for life. He *is* Kansas basketball.

Jeff Boschee

It was after my sophomore year, and I was running back and forth between Lawrence and North Dakota, doing basketball camps. I didn't really hear anything about Coach Williams and the North Carolina coaching job until I was in Smith Center, Kansas, doing a camp. A reporter from out there came up and asked me, "Did you hear about Coach Williams leaving for North Carolina?" I was like, "What?" I really didn't get any other particulars, being out in Western Kansas. They don't get much media stuff out there. I called my mom to get more information. I guess the newspapers in North Carolina were saying that he signed a contract for seven years or something like that. I really didn't know what to believe.

I found out that he hadn't accepted the job yet; he was still deciding. I really thought deep down that he wouldn't take the job, because I felt his loyalties to his players and the program would stand in the end. When he came to our house to recruit me, he told me and my parents that he would be at Kansas all four years. That was one of the things I was looking for when I was recruited. I really felt that his loyalty would stand through, and it did.

I knew the night before he announced he was staying. Kenny Gregory and I were up in Marysville, Kansas. I hadn't been back to Lawrence yet; I had been doing camps all over the state. Kenny told me that he had talked to Coach Williams the day before he got up to Marysville, and that he was staying. I was pretty relieved.

Kevin Pritchard

That was tough, the probation following the '88 championship, because when I went to college, I

Kevin Pritchard (Lawrence Journal-World)

had a couple of goals. Number one was to play in four NCAA tournaments, and because of the probation, we couldn't. What's funny now is what was said and done in terms of what we got put on probation for–today it would be a slap on the wrist. We were totally a team that they made an example out of.

I met Coach Williams the first day and really, really liked him. I didn't know how he was going to coach, obviously, but he and I ended up being great friends, and I enjoyed playing for him immensely. He's tough, but he's also fair. It was really good for me, because he's one of those coaches who really tries to instill confidence in his players. And if you come to practice and work hard every day, you've got a chance to play a lot of minutes. So it was really great for me.

My senior season, 1990, was unbelievable. Probably the best year I've ever had. The reason why, if you look at our stats, I think we had six or seven guys in double figures. We had a team that could really pass. If you go back and look at the history of Kansas basketball, I would imagine that no other team did more back doors than that team. Now I don't know that for sure, but all of us could really pass and shoot, so everybody had to really play us up. We could really pick teams apart with our offense.

Jeff Boschee

If we played well, Coach Williams was really laid-back. Still a little serious, but more laid-back. Whenever we were playing well, it always seemed like there was one thing he always wanted to correct us on. And that's just the coach trying to be perfectionist—telling us what we need and what we have to do. Other than that, there would be a lot of compliments, and just to make sure we kept playing hard in the second half.

Sometimes when you're up on a team 30 points in the first half, it's hard to beat them by 30 points in the second half. We'd try to start to beat them, just by handling the second half like we did the first half, and it's hard to keep that concentration level up there. Generally, most of the things he said were positive.

Coach Williams had some weird superstitions about pouring, how the managers poured their cokes before the game. We always said the Lord's Prayer before each game. He was probably more superstitious than any of us on the team. He was always doing something with superstitions or rituals.

Adonis Jordan

Yeah, Coach Williams is superstitious. He talks about how he wears the same suit sometimes, or the same tie, and at different times he will mention it to us. He probably had a thousand different things he could do, probably at home that we didn't know about. He was always into "whatever's working, don't change it."

He never really got emotional before a game, and he didn't really focus on the other team. His thing was this: Were we ready and prepared for that game? He was pretty calm in the locker room before the game. Now halftime was a different story, depending on which way the game was going. If he felt we weren't playing to our potential and giving our max, his voice might raise a couple of notches to get our attention. He was always a coach who encourages. He made us feel like as long as we played hard, it was okay to make mistakes, as long as they were aggressive mistakes and we were playing hard. He never wanted us to play timid.

I learned a lot from him on the court and off the court. The most important things were off the court. I'm a young man, a responsible young man, and he instilled the importance of family values, loving your family and stuff like that. He definitely put that in our systems.

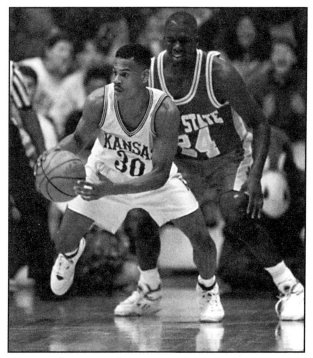

Adonis Jordan (Lawrence Journal-World)

Coach is very traditional. I've noticed that he's loosened up a lot just from watching him on TV now. And he's loosened the guys up a lot. I guess they have a little more freedom now when they play. With us he was really, really strict. We had to play a certain way, and that pretty much was it. Sometimes some of the guys didn't like it, sometimes we just felt like we strained to do our thing, but in the long run, we'd win.

Nick Bradford

Coach Williams would scream a little bit, but I think every year he didn't scream and yell as much as he did when I first got there. I don't know what it was

Nick Bradford (University of Kansas Archives)

that caused the change. He'd yell at you pretty good, but he chose different individuals, because some guys can take it and deal with it more than others. He had some pretty good judgment on that. He just did the right thing to push each individual's buttons. He was very good at giving us certain scenarios to motivate us, or maybe how Dean Smith used to do some things.

Just Relax

The 2001-02 Jayhawks appeared to be a looser group, a little more relaxed than some of Roy Williams's previous teams.

"I think the kids are more relaxed than other teams," Williams said of his '02 team. "I know I'm more relaxed. I think there is always a sense of getting that from the coach or from the coaching staff. It just makes good articles, good press I guess, to say that those other teams felt pressure and in fact the only team that I've ever coached that I thought felt the pressure and that pressure caused us to play poorly, or poorly enough to lose, was in 1990." The 1990 Jayhawks won their first 19 games and went from being unranked to number one in the country. They finished the season with a 30-5 record, and lost to UCLA in the second round of the NCAA Tournament.

"In 1997 I didn't think that team felt pressure and played poorly because of that. We were banged up, Arizona played a great game, that kind of thing," Williams said of possibly his strongest squad at KU. "In 1998 we were banged up even more, and Rhode Island had a couple guys–and one of them is still doing it in the NBA right now that people didn't know that much about, but Cutino Mobley played an outstanding game against us. I don't know that those teams in '97 or '98 did–I don't think that pressure had anything to do at all with us losing. In 1990 it did. I thought those kids cared so much and worried so much about what people were thinking that the pressure did get to them.

"[The 2002 team], they're a lot more relaxed, and I think they've been that way the whole year and yet when they go out there and lace 'em up, they get after it pretty doggone well and things don't frustrate them very often during games. We'll have some bad possessions or bad minutes, but over the course of 40 minutes they're able to hold their focus pretty well."

The 2002 Jayhawks finished with a 33-4 record and lost to Maryland in the national semifinals at the Final Four in Atlanta.

Adonis Jordan

At least once a year, Coach Williams would throw the whole team out of practice. Sometimes he might do it just to shake it up some, especially if he felt we were being too lazy or getting too big-headed. He'd do that just to let us know who the boss was and put us back on track.

Jeff Boschee

One thing Coach Williams does is to put us in a position to make a play and score. We always have an inside option first; our second option is always going to be for someone else to come off the screen and shoot. He really gives us options at both ends. I think this place is a great program for a big man to come in and play–if you watched Drew Gooden and Nick Collison develop through their years–because Coach Williams is a big man's coach. He really works hard with those guys, not that he takes anything away from the perimeter guys, because they get just as much attention. But his first option is always get the ball inside, and that's obviously the smartest thing to do. It's a lot easier to make a layup than a three-pointer.

Our practices were pretty intense. If you weren't getting out there or you weren't giving everything you had–not concentrating and being mentally into practice–he'd let you know about it. In the four years I was at KU, I think he trusted the team my senior year [2002] a lot more than he did in the years past. You could really tell by the way practices were, which were considerably shorter from years in the past. We'd go from a two-hour practice to some practices that were only 45 minutes, an hour on the court. I think he really trusted this team, and we proved to him that when we came to practice, we were ready to work.

He always told us, "You guys keep working hard in practice and showing up in the game competing, playing smart, you'll have the mental toughness to win." We did that, and I think we kept his trust pretty much the whole season.

Greg Gurley

There are two different Coach Williamses at the half during a game if we're behind. There's the Coach Williams who'll come in ranting and raving, throwing stuff, getting in your face, pumping his fist–that kind of stuff. Then there's the disappointed Coach Williams who comes in with kind of a sad face and just looks at you with an honest approach and says, "Hey, I don't know what to do, guys. I've done everything I can do. You're just going to have to go out there and do it." It's kind of like when your parents say "I'm disappointed in you." or "You failed me." More than ranting and raving and throwing stuff–which gets you motivated for a while–but then you still have to go out and maintain that for 20 minutes.

Roy Williams barks instructions to his team during a game in 1998. (Lawrence Journal-World)

The two different Coach Williamses is kind of the thing that I look back on that you never know what you're going to get. You could be getting beat by 15 points and he'll come in there and very calmly go over the stats, talk about what you're doing wrong, and just say, "Hey, look, we've got to play better. We are better, and we can beat this team." And when he did that, it was usually more beneficial and motivational than throwing the Gatorade jug, but both things have to happen throughout the year. You can't do one or the other all the time, and he understands that.

In my four-year career, Coach Williams cursed maybe, I don't know, 10-15 times. So you knew when he cursed that you were in trouble, you better get out there and do something. That's the amazing thing about him. Nothing against Bobby Knight, but he curses all the time and gets mad at his players. Coach Williams curses very, very little and gets the same effort. Different approaches by different guys. It works for both of them, because Bob Knight's one of the best coaches I've ever seen. He has one approach, and Coach Williams has an entirely different one.

CHAPTER 9

Tourney Time

The Jayhawks and the NCAA Tournament have become synonymous with one another. Kansas has appeared in the NCAA's big dance 31 times, advanced to the Final Four 11 times, and earned the crown of national champions twice. The Jayhawks have played in tournament games as far west as Seattle and Eugene, Oregon, and as far east as Winston Salem, North Carolina. With an impressive overall tournament record of 65-31, KU has one of the top winning percentages of any school in postseason play. Many of the program's greatest moments, as well as a few disappointments and heartbreakers, have happened to the Jayhawks during postseason play.

Dave Robisch

The 1971 Final Four was the first one played in a dome, the Astrodome. Unfortunately, they put the floor out in the middle of the Astrodome, and it was an elevated floor. I can remember the bench and the coaching staff sitting with their face at floor level watching the game. That floor was probably, I don't know, three or four feet above the ground. So that was a unique experience. They did put some bleachers around the floor, but a lot of the fans were up in the stadium's stands, and their view was terrible. And the lighting. They had lights on each corner of the floor, and if you came down at a certain angle and looked to shoot at the basket, you would see lights glaring at you in the background.

I was really excited about the challenge because I didn't like some of the remarks that came out of the West Coast on UCLA. We were 27-1, just like they were, and they thought that they were going to be the superior team. Supposedly they were going to use their quickness and superior athletic ability and it was not going to be a contest. I was just looking forward to the challenge. We were probably getting nervous and tight a little bit because it had been such a tough journey to get there. But I think those experiences along the way prepared us for that situation.

Bud Stallworth

We were really tripping by the time we headed to Houston for the Final Four in 1971. We came back after the regionals and Lawrence was rocking. Our heads were so big we probably couldn't walk through a door. The football players threw a big party for us. The guy who ran the training table put a spread together that most professional teams don't see. It was unbelievable, the town, the state, everything was Jayhawks. The first practice after we got back from the regionals, Coach Miranda tried to bring us back to earth. "Get on the line and start running. Do another one for UCLA. Do one for Sidney Wicks. Do one for Henry Bibby. Get back to work. You lucked through the Regionals; now we have to get back to work and get out

Aubrey Nash, Dave Robisch, Bud Stallworth and Pierre Russell celebrate after the Jayhawks win the 1971 NCAA Midwest Regional. (University of Kansas Archives)

there and win this thing." There was no fear about playing UCLA. We couldn't wait to get to Houston.

When we got to the Astrodome before the game, we were ready to bite the bars off the lockers. We were ready to get out there and play. Everybody was pumped. We had a TV monitor in the locker room and we were watching the first semifinal game, Western Kentucky against Villanova. They were battling; it was one of those tight games, nip and tuck all the way. We had gone through our pregame scouting reports, the normal psyche-up routine, and Coach Owens's speech.

We were ready to blast through the door. Just get it on, take our shot. We were ready to roll out onto the court! And Western Kentucky and Villanova go into overtime. That just blew our whole adrenaline thing away. The edge, for us, was to get out there while we had that momentum thing ready. I think that kind of hurt us in the beginning, having to sit through an overtime. We had that psyche thing going, lost it, and then had to get it back. It was probably a little easier for UCLA because they'd been there before. I don't think we came out as sharp as we would have been if we'd come out at the end of the regulation game instead of after the overtime.

The game started, and I got hurt. Hurt my leg probably in the first couple of minutes. It was a freak kind of thing, too. They were pressing us, and I was getting ready to go into one of my lanes that I needed to be in, and I tripped, hit this guy. His knee hit my shin, and I thought he broke my leg. A knot popped up, and Dean Nesmith, our trainer, put some of that freeze stuff on it. But even with that and a couple of questionable calls, we settled down and got into the game with them. It was a good game. They won, we lost. That's the way it is, and I wasn't real happy. I think if we played them again, we'd probably beat them, could have split ten games with them, going five and five.

Paul Mokeski

Instead of playing in Wichita and then at home for the NCAA Tournament in 1978, they sent us out to the West Coast to play UCLA in Oregon. It was disappointing, but it was also exciting for me because I grew up a Bruins fan. Back then, not all the games were on TV. There wasn't "Crazy Tuesday" and "Manic Monday." There was one regional game and one national game on a week. That was all. I knew my family and friends and people I'd grown up with were going to get to see this game.

It was kind of a neat arena at Oregon. We played really well for most of the game and actually took a lead, I think

Paul Mokeski (University of Kansas Archives)

10 or 12 points. We had control of that game, but then there were some suspicious calls by the officials. All of a sudden, we have Ken Koenigs, Darnell [Valentine] and Clint Johnson with four fouls. Back then, there was no shot clock. When we wanted to ice a game, we'd go into a four-corner offense with Darnell handling the ball. I remember sitting in the huddle and Coach Owens was saying, "Now we're going to go into our four corners" or whatever we called it back then. But we were all pumped up. "No. Let's run them out of here. We're going to blow this thing wide open."

Instead of going into the four corners, we just kept playing ball. And eventually, I was the only starter still in the game, but I fouled out, too.

I don't know what we lost by. I remember I had 18 points, and I was the first player on a non-winning team to win the TV Player of the Game.

What Do You Think of Us Now?

Following the Jayhawks' win over Oklahoma to capture the 1988 NCAA championship, Danny Manning had a few words for KU's pre-tournament detractors.

"It's a great feeling and something we deserved," Manning said. "How do you think this feels, to win a championship and finish your career in Kansas City in front of the people who've supported you for four years? A lot of people said we were lucky, but what's luck? Luck is when preparation meets opportunity.

"To all the people who said we were finished, we're national champions, and what do you think of us now?"

B. H. Born

During the finals of the NCAA Tournament in 1953, I had a real bad head cold, and it had settled in my inner ears. I was going to the doctor and they were draining my ears with a pump. I was having trouble with my equilibrium, and that's kind of bad when you're trying to rebound—you don't know which way is up.

I came to the dressing room at the half and said to our trainer, Dean Nesmith, "Deaner, I'm really stopped up. Do you have anything to gargle?" He said, "No, all I have is alum water." I didn't know what it was, but I took a little of

Danny Manning (University of Kansas Archives)

the alum water and tried to gargle it. Doc Allen saw me doing that and said, "How can you be an All-American if you don't even know how to gargle?" He grabbed me by the back of the hair, pulled my head back and I swallowed the alum water, which had a very bitter taste. Doc Allen went on with his instructions.

"You stand with your feet 18 inches apart and pull your head back." Then he pulled my head back again and said, "Now gargle." He spent more than half the damn half-time teaching me how to gargle, *and we were playing Indi-*

ana in the finals of the NCAA. Coach Harp finally drew up a couple of things on the chalkboard just minutes before we went back out for the second half of the game.

In the second half, the official scorer messed up the number of fouls I had, and when I committed my fourth foul, they said I had five. Branch McCracken, the Indiana coach, went over to the scorer and said, "Get him out of there." They stopped the game for about five minutes. Of course, we kept track of my fouls, because Al Kelly and I fouled out of about every game. I think he led the country, and I was real close behind him in number of fouls. Anyway, they polled all of the sportswriters, and all of them held up their hands showing they had me down for four fouls. McCracken pounded on that table and said, "I don't give a damn how many sportswriters say he's got four fouls, the official scorer is the one you count. Now get him out of there!"

The president of the NCAA came down and said I only had four fouls. They finally figured out that one of Jerry Alberts's fouls had been given to me, and that's why I had five. They took it off mine and put it back on his. I did eventually foul out, but I was the MVP of the Final Four. I fouled out with a minute and a half to go and we were ahead, but we ended up losing by one point.

Anti-Arkansas T-shirt Banned

Following their 93-81 victory over the Arkansas Razorbacks to capture the 1991 Southeast Regional title, KU players donned championship T-shirts celebrating the win. The shirt had "Arkansas" across the front, but the "Ar" had a red circle around it and slash through it, turning the word into "Kansas." Unfortunately, the shirt broke a

KU licensing policy that prohibits derogatory connotations of other universities on the same item with a KU logo.

There was a big demand by KU fans for the shirt, but only a few people actually got one. A local Lawrence store had printed some shirts following the Jayhawks' win, but after the university asked them to stop selling them, they did.

Maybe Roy Williams summed up the situation concerning the T-shirts better than anyone else.

"I think it's silly," he said of the illegal T-shirts.

Chris Piper

Our 1986 team was better, but the 1988 team won. The '88 team wasn't as good as the '86 team by any means, but that's what the NCAA Tournament is all about. That was just a great, great team in 1986. The thing was, we still didn't have 100 percent confidence going in. It is unbelievable to this day that a team that has that many wins didn't win it all, but it was the first time in the Final Four for all of us. I think we were walking on eggshells against Duke in that game in 1986. I think, and I say this all the time, if we would have won in 1986, number one, Danny [Manning] might not have been in school in '88, and it is likely we wouldn't have won in 1988. But the fact that we went to the Final Four 1986 helped us win in 1988–Danny and I had been there. There are so many distractions in the Final Four and if you're not used to it, you can let those things get in the way of your game, easily lose sight of what's really important. For us in '88, that was a huge contributing factor. It was just another game for us and we were going out to play. The fact we were playing in Kansas City and a huge underdog–nobody thought we could win anyway– really helped us as well.

Chris Piper battles Oklahoma's Stacy King during the 1988 NCAA Championship game. (Lawrence Journal-World)

Looking back at the clock game against Michigan State in the 1986 Midwest Regional, I think we actually got penalized more for it because Coach Brown got a technical for coming out, trying to figure out what Jud Heathcote, the Michigan State coach, was doing. They got points and the ball back. The clock stopping was really a moot point. We were extremely fortunate in that game because they missed free throws. I was in the game at the end as a defensive sub, and Michigan State's Scott Skiles had the floor spread. He's the only guy that ever matched Calvin Thompson for talking trash on the floor—he and Calvin were going back and forth the whole game. Calvin was a big trash talker, all-time king of the trash talking as far as I'm concerned. Nothing derogatory or anything like that, but he was good at it. Still, Scott Skiles gave him his money's worth, so to speak, and Calvin kind of liked it, too. They were having fun going back and forth. Anyway, they had the floor spread against us, and I was guarding their best free-throw shooter. I saw the clock going down, and I finally made up my mind, "I've got to foul," and I did. The guy missed both of them. We had a timeout right after that, and Coach Brown looked at me and said, "Pipe, you're really lucky. He's their best free-throw shooter." Which I didn't happen to know at the time. So that worked out well for us. He missed the free throws or I would have been in big trouble. And we were able to win the game in overtime.

If you watch the Duke-Kansas game from the Final Four in '86, you'll see that both teams played poorly. It was an ugly game, and either team could have won. I think losing Archie Marshall in that game sapped something out of us. I'm not sure if that took more out of us or losing Danny to fouls took more out of us. We were in bad foul trouble, it seemed, for the entire game.

Game Winner or Out of Bounds?

The 1966 Midwest Regional Championship game had come down to this: with seven seconds remaining in overtime, Texas Western and KU were tied at 71 all, and the Jayhawks had the ball. Jo Jo White took the inbounds pass from his backcourt mate, Delvey Lewis, and turned up the floor. He was forced to the left sideline, looked up and saw that three seconds remained on the clock. White pivoted on his right foot, moved his left foot backwards slightly, and let fly a 30-foot jump shot.

The ball fell through the net, and the Jayhawks thought they were in the Final Four.

"When I released the ball I backed up and sat on this lady's lap," White said of his apparent game-winning shot. "Bobby Joe Hill [of Texas Western] had jumped, trying to block the shot, and hit me on the arm. I thought the official was calling a foul, but when he came out of the backcourt, he said my foot was on the out-of-bounds line." The shot was disallowed, of course, and the game went into a second overtime.

"I was in bounds," White said. "We watched the game film over and over and it showed I was in. [Going into the second overtime] we were still there in the game. We felt it was our game to win. My spirits were high; I wasn't down at all."

"We didn't realize he was even that close to the side-line," KU coach Ted Owens said of the shot. "Even today there is some question as to whether he was out or not."

Texas Western would hold off the Jayhawks in the second overtime and win the game, 81-80.

"It was hard to get settled down after you think you had the game won," Owens said. "As it turned out, we would have been better off if Jo Jo hadn't made it [the shot], because going into the second overtime it was like we had just had it stolen away from us."

"All of my memories of that game go right back to that one particular shot," White said. "Had it counted, we would have been on the other side of the spectrum. They're fond

Was he in or out? Jo Jo White prepares to shoot what would have been the game-winning shot against Texas Western in the 1966 NCAA Midwest Regional Championship game. The official ruled White stepped out of bounds. KU lost in double overtime, 81-80.
(University of Kansas Archives)

memories, but on the other hand, they're kind of disappointing because of that shot."

"We had a few times when we were close to winning the championship," Owens recalled of his career at KU, "and 1966 certainly was maybe the closest we came. It was a great team."

Tony Guy

My big game against Arizona State in the 1981 NCAA Tournament–I scored 36 points–just kind of happened. As talented as ASU was, they didn't play hard on defense. For the most part, I was shooting wide-open jump shots and thinking, "When are they going to come out and guard us?" I don't know if they just felt that no matter how many points we scored, they would score more or if they thought, "We're better than this team and can just turn it up a notch at any time and blow these guys away." Whatever it was, they couldn't come back.

I'll never forget after the game, we were walking out to get on our team bus, and they were already on their bus and about to leave. Those guys were laughing and joking and saying, "Hey, you all killed us. You all blew us out." I'll never forget that. It was as if they were going home to a big party, life was just a big bowl of cherries. It was the weirdest thing I've ever seen. You would have never known, by looking at them anyway, that those guys had just lost.

During the game, it was a neat deal that I got into a rhythm. Darnell [Valentine] recognized that I was in rhythm, my other teammates recognized I was in a rhythm, and it just seemed like I was in the zone. It was a nationally televised game, and I knew my family and all my friends back in Baltimore were watching. There was a play in the first half when Arizona State had scored against us and we had taken it down real quick. I was running down the left side of the floor, wide open. Darnell saw me and threw me the ball. I took a couple dribbles, and when I got to the free-throw line, I took off. I'm in the air and I'm thinking, "Yeah, Tony, this is great. You're about to embarrass yourself on national TV. There's no way you're going to get to the rim from how far out you took off. You're going to fall on your face on national TV." But for some strange reason, I just kept going, and going, and I got to the basket and I dunked it. I was shocked and I tried not to let everybody know how shocked I was.

Tony Guy (Hank Young)

I was fouled on the play, too. I got to the team huddle before I shot the free throw and those guys were looking at me like, "You okay, man? We've never seen you dunk a basketball shot like that before." I'm trying to keep my game face on, but I'm still thinking to myself, "I can't believe I got away with that."

To go from that to the Wichita State game–apparently Wichita State felt that KU had avoided scheduling them over the years–was strange. It became an extremely personal game. That particular year Wichita State had a good basketball team. Those guys could flat-out play. We played well, but they made some shots that if they had to do over again, there's no way. But that's why we play the game, because you never know what's going to happen. They made the shots when they needed to make them. It was a good basketball game, but they ended up winning, 66-65. It was definitely a terrible way to end the season.

Adonis Jordan

Going to the Final Four in 1991 was amazing. It was amazing because we weren't really supposed to be there. We upset a couple of teams to get there, and from the second round on when we played Pittsburgh, we were the underdog. Then we played Indiana and we were the underdog. We had Arkansas, that's when they had their big guys, and we were a big underdog and beat them. When we played North Carolina in the Final Four, we were the underdog. And we beat them to go to the finals.

After our game against Arkansas, I said "Down by 12, win by 12." That was exciting, because we weren't supposed to win. We were down by 12 at the half, and they had pretty much penciled us out. That was one of the halftimes when Coach Williams's voice went up a few notches. He let us know that we weren't playing to our potential. We just came out in the second half, picked it up and ended up winning by 12.

When we played North Carolina in the Final Four in 1991 there was a lot of added emotion, simply because Coach Williams was [at UNC] for so many years, and they ran the same exact thing we ran, even down to the warmups and the layup line. Basically, it was like this: whichever team executed the best was going to win that game, whichever team made the least mistakes was the team that was going to come out on top. And that time, we did.

Because we played the first game at the 1991 Final Four, and after we won, we just knew in our hearts that we were going to play UNLV, the top-rated team in the country. They went undefeated that year. I guess when Duke won, we got a little too confident. I think we relaxed, not a lot, but just human nature-type of relaxing. The big top dog wasn't there anymore, so it would be easier to get to the championship. I tell everybody that I wish we would have played UNLV because the way the tournament was going, we were the underdog every single time. When we played Duke, we might still have been the underdog, but it was more like nobody really knew who could win. If we could have played UNLV, it would have been like all the other games and we'd have been a big-time underdog.

Kevin Pritchard

The funny thing about [1988] is when we were talking about going to the tournament, it was more like, "Okay, we've got this tournament. Let's hopefully have a good chance of winning it." For me, it was more just wanting to play well versus "Boy, we really need to win this thing." We had the attitude of just playing, and then seeing what happens. Because of that, I think there weren't the expectations on ourselves that some teams have.

Before the K-State game for the Midwest Regional championship, Coach Brown said, "Let's go out and have some fun. Let's play like we've been playing." We knew each other so well by then that it was just a matter of who could stop our strengths and who could maximize on our weaknesses. Because of that, it was a fun game, a back-and-forth game. We pulled away at the end and won, 71-58.

I think the most important thing before we played Duke in the Final Four was that we didn't feel pressure. We weren't worried about, "Oh my gosh, if we don't win ..." We just went out and played. Because of that, I think it gave us an advantage over everybody else. That team didn't get tight.

Jeff Boschee

Playing in the Final Four, that's something every little kid dreams about as they grow up wanting to play any type of basketball. The Final Four was something else. Seeing 60,000 people sitting there watching you—and some 20,000 watching you practice is even more unreal. Just the hard work I put in for those three, three and a half years, just to know that the payoff came so close to winning the national title.

I don't think we got nervous in the Maryland game. I think we got outplayed in every aspect of the game. We had a big letdown there at the beginning of the second half. Maryland is a team where you can't let down at any point. I didn't think they were that much better than us, if they were better than us, but they were better on that night for sure. I don't think we played up to par, but we didn't give up and came back to really make a game out of it. You have got to give a lot of credit to them, though.

Mike Maddox

I had two completely different experiences in the Final Four. In 1988 I was a freshman, and I didn't have a clue as to what to expect. It was unique in '88 because we were in Kansas City and we were such a Cinderella team that year, even more so than in 1991. There weren't a lot of expectations. We just kind of really came together as a team, and we knew that if we played well, we could beat anybody. We had a guy like Danny on the team that could put us on his back and carry us. It also was unique because in '88 we ended up playing teams that we had played before in the tournament. We played K-State, Duke, and Oklahoma, and we knew we could play with those teams.

In 1991, we weren't expected to get to the Final Four, either. We were a No. 3 seed, I think. Again, we just started clicking as a team. We didn't have any superstars, but we had a lot of guys who knew their roles, and we really executed well. One could argue that in '91 we had a tougher road than we did in '88. We had to beat Indiana, Arkansas—the No. 1 seed, No. 2 seed—then we had North Carolina, another No. 1 seed, and finally, Duke, who beat us. That team really came together and again got hot at the right time. I also think the experience we went through in '88 helped us in '91 because Mark Randall and I, at least, had been there before and kind of knew what to expect.

Greg Gurley

When we were upset by UTEP in 1992, there was disappointment. There was shock. There was just confusion. Everyone was talking about us. We were a great, great team that season. There were some tears in the locker room. To see big, strong men crying, I don't know. We had Alonzo Jamison, who was a senior on the team, a few other guys. It opened your eyes up, knowing you had to come and do it every night. That was about our 35th game of the year, and we knew that, but when it ultimately hits, it's just utter disappointment, confusion, frustration and shock, all in one.

The Final Four in 1993 was just unreal. It was in a perfect city, New Orleans. You get down there and it's just nuts. It was the one and only time I've been to New Orleans, and people always talk about Mardi Gras and everything. ESPN followed us around, kind of walking up and down Bourbon Street. Every move we made, people were watching us. As a Kansas basketball player, you get used to that to an extent. But when this is it, when that's the big stage, the only thing going on, it was a little overwhelming at first to go out there on Friday and have a practice with what seemed like 20-25,000 people watching us. And there were 60,000 some at the game.

To put a basketball court in a football stadium and fill pretty much every seat–it was just amazing. I had ticket requests from all over, family and friends, everybody wanted tickets. My parents only missed three of my games in my entire college career, so they were there in force. It was a lot of fun. Even though we lost, which was very disappointing, it was something that I will never forget. Every once in a while, I'll put that Final Four ring on at a sports function or a black tie affair, and it's pretty neat.

Roger Morningstar

Playing in the Final Four was one of those things that didn't really hit us until afterwards. No one thought we had the wherewithal to pull that off at the start of our season, anyway. As things went on, we weren't taken quite so lightly and we didn't take ourselves quite so lightly. So we felt like we had a shot at it, but when the reality sets in, there's a lot of combination of playing well and having a lot of luck that'll get you into that. It's just not as easy as it might seem, even with really great players, to get to the Final Four. There's always somebody playing an incredible game against you, or something that doesn't allow you to go. Although in the back of our minds, in 1974, we never thought we could achieve something like that. It was a pleasant surprise when we did, a huge feeling. That was a long night of celebration in the hotel after we beat ORU to go, and there was a strong group of Kansans down there because it wasn't that far away. We had a great time.

The Final Four then, although it was a big deal from a basketball standpoint, it was nothing like the circus it is today. There wasn't that much media. We stayed in a Holiday Inn–they put those little letters up on the sign outside: Welcome Kansas Jayhawks–played at the Greensboro Coliseum in North Carolina. It just wasn't as big a circus as it is today. It's hard to find the teams that are playing in it today; they're all staying in hotels on private floors, with security all around. There are nine million media people, events for

Roger Morningstar (Lawrence Journal-World)

the fans to go to. It's a week-long extravaganza today, and back then, it was only a big deal basketball-wise. That was it. You showed up, played the games, and boom, it's over.

We were excited, went down there and didn't play very well. Marquette beat us in the semifinal game by 13 points. I know we were disappointed about that because they were a team that we felt we could compete with. They had a couple kids who had career games, and of course, Al McGuire was their coach. He was always good for something.

The two losers of the semifinal games, UCLA and us, had to play in the meaningless consolation game. UCLA lost an incredible game to North Carolina State. It was just an incredible battle and UCLA had about five chances to win; they just found a way to lose it. They had made noise that they weren't going to play the consolation game. There was no sense in it, and why? They ended beating us pretty bad in that game. I don't know if that was the last year for the consolation game, but it wasn't too long after that that they stopped playing it.

The Final Four was a very cool thing, and not very many teams get to go to the Final Four when you look at the big picture. There are an awful lot of players, teams and coaches who never make it to that thing. It's some great memories, and we were just glad to be able to add a little bit to the Kansas tradition that has always been so strong.

Nick Bradford

My preparation wasn't the same for the NCAA Tournament–I put more emphasis on little things. That was one of the biggest things, just emphasis on boxing out, doing the little things and kind of letting people know where you'll be on the court, more so than any other time during the season. You just try to play your best ball during tournament time.

When we prepared for Arizona in 1997, we were pretty confident. We'd had a good win against Purdue; it was a tough game. But we thought we were the best team in basketball. We knew Arizona was good, but we thought we were ready. They were quick, but we weren't surprised. They just executed better than we did that day.

The biggest disappointment about that loss was that Jacque Vaughn and Jerod Haase hadn't gone to the Final

Four starters on the 1997 KU team are now in the NBA. From the left, Paul Pierce, Scot Pollard, Jacque Vaughn and Raef LaFrentz. (Lawrence Journal-World)

Four. They really wanted to go, especially since we were the best team in the country.

After winning 30-plus games that year, we had a lot of experience and a lot of clutch moments of decision making. We knew how to make good decisions in different situations. Paul Pierce, Raef LaFrentz, Scot Pollard, Jacque and Jerod were great teammates. I lived with Paul and I lived with Raef, so I knew them pretty well. They were great teammates and taught us to strive to be better.

Gooden at the Final Four

When you're an All-American at the Final Four, it's a good bet that you'll be showered with attention, from fans and media alike. Drew Gooden received that kind of attention at the 2002 Final Four.

"It has been fun," Gooden said of his Final Four experience, before the Jayhawks lost to Maryland in the national semifinals. "A lot of students have congratulated us on what we have accomplished and there are a lot of people that are happy that we are in the Final Four. The celebration could be more than in other places, but Lawrence is a college town and has a big basketball tradition. There will be a lot of fun times and wild times around this city."

Another Upset Loss

Roy Williams's teams have been victimized several times by underdogs in the NCAA Tournament. In 1998, the Jayhawks were again sent packing by a supposedly lesser team, Rhode Island.

"About the only way to handle this type of disappointment is to try to work as hard as I can," Williams said shortly after KU lost to Rhode Island in the second round of the '98 tournament. "The more I sit around, it bothers me too much. I had a visit on Monday with a prospect. I went recruiting yesterday. I'm going recruiting this afternoon. I'm going to try to enjoy life and go be a dad tomorrow . . . It is hard. We had some goals. We had some dreams that we were not able to reach. You think about 35-4 and winning the league. We won the league seven of the last eight years. We won the title by four full games. We won the conference tournament for the second year in a row. The first time that has ever been done. So we have some great memories. I push our team all of the time and try to push our fans to enjoy the journey. I probably enjoyed the journey that this team took me on as much if not more than any team I have ever had. Getting Wilt Chamberlain to come back and retire his jersey, the reunion, the home-court winning streak. There were so many great experiences and great times. And yet, at the end of the year, I've described it before, it is like somebody pulled my heart out and shook it right in front of my face and taunted me. It's hard. I'm too emotional."

Bob Billings

We came back to the campus after losing to North Carolina because there was a big dance. It was a very sad bus ride coming back from Kansas City. Louis Armstrong was playing at the dance, and we were introduced then. I think everybody thought that we had an awful good chance to win. But North Carolina played smart and played well.

At that particular time, it was Coach Harp's first year, and I think he was still feeling his way. I was around the team quite a bit after I graduated and in the locker room at halftimes. And at that point in time, three or four years into the job, Dick was getting very emotional with the team and was really into it. When we were sophomores and juniors, it was more a technical situation with him, and there wasn't a lot of emotion.

The emotion that was generated from our bench came from our trainer, Dean Nesmith. Deaner was very emotional, hated the officials and wanted to win in the worst way. He lived with his heart on his sleeve–a dear, dear person. I think Deaner got all but one or two of the technicals that we got as a team during my three years of play, because he was just so emotional and into the game and the officials could always hear his voice. Deaner was one of the great competitors that has ever been around KU's athletic program. He was special, and I loved him dearly.

John Parker

Playing the games in Dallas for the Midwest Regional in 1957 was a terrible experience because we had two black players, Wilt and Maurice King. The people were just wild and crazy about the way they treated Wilt and Maurice. In the first game there, we played SMU. They had a new arena, and the crowd threw coins, seat cushions and everything on the floor–all because of our black players. Finally, their athletic director came out and said, "If this doesn't stop immediately, the game will be forfeited to the University of Kansas." We continued the game, and they didn't throw anything else.

We went ahead and finished the game and ended up beating SMU. In fact, of all the teams we played on the way to the championship game, they were the best team we played. I thought they were better than North Carolina. Then in the next game, we played Oklahoma City University, and they did everything they could to try and hurt Wilt. They'd jump in front of him and try to make him fall over them. It was a terrible deal. We ended up winning and beat them rather easily.

In the game against North Carolina in the final, we didn't lose; we had it taken away from us because of the officiating. On one play, Wilt scored, dunking the ball, but they said he stepped out of bounds. Well, he didn't step out of bounds. And then the other thing that really cost us the game was–we were in the third overtime, I think it was–and they took a shot, and I got the rebound. But they called a foul on Maurice King. He was on the other side of the floor, wasn't close to anybody where they called the foul. Of course they made their free throws, and we lost the game by one point. I'll never get over that game because we should have won. And I don't know what happened.

Wilt Chamberlain fights for a rebound with an SMU player during first-round action at the 1957 NCAA tournament. (University of Kansas Archives)

Basketball is a very easy game to fix if you've got the players, but the easiest way to fix a basketball game is with officials. They can make one or two critical calls and change the whole game. In my mind, I think that's what happened. Of course, you can't prove it and never will. But it's too bad we lost that game because of those two calls.

It was a great game, but in my mind, we had the best team, and if we played them 10 times, I think we'd win eight out of 10 games. I really feel that, because we had the best players in the country, and Wilt was so much better than anybody else.

Chris Piper

We were a smart team in 1988, smart enough to know where our bread and butter was. Danny [Manning] was going to be the guy that was going to get us there. We knew that. The guys we had on that team at the end of '88–I always regretted that we never took a team picture at the end–were committed to winning. Every guy who played on that team would do anything it took to win.

I knew, for me, every time I touched the ball, I had to get it to Danny or find a way to get him open and that was what would help us win and to play defense. And Pritchard, he knew what he had to do. He would bring the ball down the floor and he'd hit shots when he needed to. But he wouldn't force the issue. Jeff Gueldner was a lot like me as well. Jeff could hit shots when he needed to, but he knew that wasn't what he was supposed to do on the floor. Milt [Newton] knew he needed to be a scorer and take pressure off Danny and, again, play defense. Everybody bought into Coach Brown's defensive concept. You know, the thing is, I know a lot of guys who will talk about that '88 championship game, saying, "Danny got all the credit for that, and look at rest of you guys, shooting something like 75 percent from the floor." I always say, "Yeah, but we wouldn't have been shooting 75 percent from the floor if Danny hadn't been out there drawing the defense off us." Danny, rightfully so, was the story. I do take a little offense when I hear

Jubilant Kansas players celebrate following their upset win over Oklahoma in the 1988 NCAA Championship game. (Susan Ragan, AP/Wide World Photos)

people talk about how he put the team on his shoulders and carried it, because that really wasn't the case. And Danny would never say that was the case either. But there's no way in the world we'd even come close without Danny. I would like to think that the guys who were on that team were smart enough to do the things to help Danny win the national championship, because he wouldn't have been able to do it without them either. That's the way it was with that team.

Another thing that sticks in my mind happened in the locker room after the championship game was over. We were all in there whooping and hollering, and Coach Brown was talking to us. The door opened and the room went silent, and you hear the unmistakable voice of Billy Tubbs, the Oklahoma coach, congratulating us, telling us what a great game we played and all that. It was just dead silence. You might not be able to fathom it. You really had to be there to understand and feel it. Tubbs finished and then turned around and walked out. Coach Brown just looked around at us and said, "Wow." That's all he said, just "Wow." It was his really big moment. I don't know why, but it really was.

Kevin Pritchard

It was a manic-depressive season, 1988. We were good, we were bad, we were good, and we were bad. We didn't know which team would show up for games. Coach Brown made a couple of changes. He made me the point guard, inserted Jeff Gueldner at the other guard, and Milt Newton was playing more minutes at small forward because of Archie Marshall's injury. It was a season where we kind of started out with one team and ended up with another one. The team really had a transformation. We went from one team at the beginning of the season to about three or four in the middle, until our final, starting team at the end.

Dave Robisch

Not to make excuses, but I think the physical set-up of the Astrodome really affected my shooting more than anything. I remember the number of shots that I took at the regional and the amount of free throws that I got were basically the same. I was looking to have the same success in Houston. And my shooting was a little bit affected by that. As I've told many, many people when I'm asked about my career, the thing that I remember most about all the success that we had at KU and getting to the Final

Archie Marshall (University of Kansas Archives)

Four in that special year was in the UCLA game in the second half. They had been ahead and we had a chance for the first time in the game to take the lead. We were one point behind, and I came down on a fast break and took a shot that I've taken in many, many games and hundreds of times in practice. I made the shot to put us ahead of UCLA, and the official called me for traveling. It was what I had done for so many times. And momentum is a funny thing. When you get ahead of a team, that's a psychological edge that I thought we had accomplished, and then it was taken away from us. Our bubble burst with that play a little bit, and we ended up losing by eight points, but I thought we had a great chance. I certainly wasn't in awe of UCLA at all. I thought we could beat them and win the national championship.

It's a special memory for me, winning the Midwest Regional in front of our fans and the State of Kansas at Wichita. KU hadn't been to the Final Four since Wilt Chamberlain, so it had been a long time. Bringing us back to that was another special thing.

I'm glad that more teams get the opportunity to play now and that March Madness is what it is today. What you have to realize is that to get to the Final Four when we played, you had to win the conference. If you didn't win the conference, you didn't qualify to go to the tournament.

To go undefeated in the Big Eight and then to win the regional to get to the Final Four under those conditions in 1971, that was one of the things I was tremendously proud of.

CHAPTER 10

The Kansas Tradition

The long and storied history of Kansas basketball is more than great coaches, number of wins, Final Fours, or national championships. More than anything else, it is about a continuous, winning tradition that dates back more than 100 years to James Naismith, the game's inventor, and Phog Allen, the school's all-time greatest coach. The players, maybe more than any other aspect of the program's success, are the ones most responsible for continuing and enhancing the legacy of the Kansas basketball tradition.

Bud Stallworth

They can talk about North Carolina, Duke and UCLA, Kentucky. But North Carolina and Kentucky got their basketball roots from KU, and there's no greater legacy in college basketball than Kansas. We might not have all the national championships that Kentucky has, that North Carolina and Duke have, but tradition-wise and being one of the lead programs in the country, we don't take a back seat to anybody. When I played, I got that special feeling about KU, and I remember thinking, "This is what I want, this is what I want it to feel like, this is why I came to the University of Kansas, because they do care about their basketball." It's a feeling I've had ever since.

Roger Morningstar

The fact that Coach Williams has been able to add to what Naismith and Phog Allen and Coach Harp, Coach Owens and Coach Brown all started is something we can all be proud of. Coach Williams has also done a good job of keeping the past players involved, with the reunions that he's had, giving us a chance to come back and be together and meet some of the guys who played long before us and who are all part of the tradition. I think every player who's played at Kansas has been in awe of those who have played before them. That's a pretty cool thing. It's a real healthy thing. It's not like one group came in here and turned the place out, that's the only good team they ever had. You go back, and Kansas has been to the Final Four eleven times. Kansas has won the conference many, many times. Coach Williams has put us in a position now where we're going to win some more national championships; it's just a matter of when. We've been knocking on the door every year, and when you knock on the door a lot, eventually they start coming to you. Overall, it's been one of the greatest experiences of my life to have been involved with KU basketball. I feel very fortunate, living in a place where I love to be and love to live, and none of that would have happened without the opportunity to play at KU.

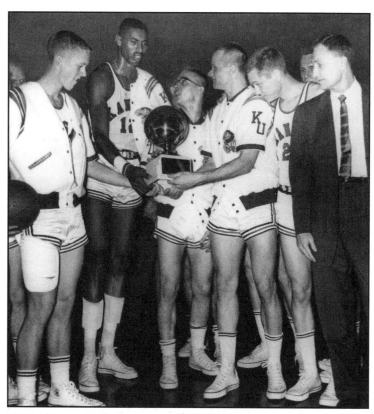

Wilt Chamberlain and Bob Billings (glasses) gather with teammates and KU coach Dick Harp (right) with the 1957 Big Eight preseason tournament trophy. (University of Kansas Archives)

Bob Billings

I've had a lot of good things happen to me in my life, but as I look back on it, athletics were very important to my maturing years, and the opportunity to play at the University of Kansas was just extraordinary. I have to thank Dr. Allen and Dick Harp for making that possible. It's a very special place. And the people that I interacted with at that time have been lifelong friends, and you just can't replace that. I'm sure that people who go to other schools have that same feeling, but for those of us who have blue blood and Jayhawk noses, we think that Kansas is pretty good.

Chris Piper

I look back now and just think about how fortunate I was. Everything that's happened in my life after that has been because of the opportunity, really, to play at KU. It's just kind of mind-boggling sometimes when I take a look at where I'm at now and the things that led up to it. How fortunate I am. I was going nowhere, and who knew where I would have ended up if Coach Brown hadn't given me a chance. I always think about it and I just feel really, really thankful. Winning a national championship put me at a level–unjustly–with a lot of great Kansas players. Because by no means was I a great player. I get embarrassed today when people–you know they do charity events and things like that–introduce me as a great Kansas player. And I'm like, "I was a very, very average ballplayer for Kansas who was lucky enough to play with one of the greatest all-time coaches, Larry Brown, and one of the greatest all-time players, Danny Manning." I'll always feel extremely fortunate that I was able to be a part of that.

Dave Robisch

I think when you spend four years of your life at a school and you really enjoyed your experience, you really do have special feelings. Especially when you played basketball at a place like KU. Kansas, in my mind, based on tradition, history, number of wins, success of the program, is definitely one of the top five programs in America, and when you become a part of the tradition, the success we had as a team when I was there, and get to the Final Four, there is definitely a lot of pride and special memories from what you've accomplished. And when you consider what was going on in the country at the time when I was playing—war protests, campus unrest, etc.—it was special to see, despite all the turmoil, that we—the basketball team—were able to bring the university back together.

Mike Maddox

It's an honor to have had the opportunity to play for KU. The history is so great, and you really realize it more after you're done than you do when you're playing. Just to be a part of that history and to have played on the same floor, wear the same jersey as so many great players who have played there before we did and after we have, it's just a great honor. You really realize that when there's the 100-Year Reunion or other reunions where a lot of those players from the past come back. Just to look around that room and look at all the people who are a part of Kansas basketball, you realize it's a very special thing.

Drew Gooden

When I was riding back from the airport with coach Matt Doherty, who was an assistant at the time, all I could see were the plain fields and I just got so bored. The drive from Kansas City to Lawrence was just so disgusting since I came from California. When I got to Lawrence I saw the 1988 championship and the 1952 championship sign on the road and that is when I started getting

Drew Gooden (University of Kansas Archives)

the big picture of what Lawrence really was. I got a better understanding of why a lot of players play here and then build houses, because it is a nice area and a nice town with Midwestern folks who are very homespun. On the ride coming here, there was no way that I would plan on living here. Three years after that drive from the airport, this is my second home.

B. H. Born

I was pleased that I'd been chosen to play at KU. You go there for a quality education, and I had good experiences with all my teachers and people I'd met. Kansas has an *esprit de corps* that you don't get at every school. I've gone to probably 78-80 schools across the country in recruiting young people for Caterpillar. I've learned that the University of Kansas is right up there at the top in many ways, not just in sports, but all around. Its programs are near the top. You start looking at education, start looking at engineering and the law school, all the different programs and the conglomerate of good people, and you realize how good it really is.

Greg Gurley

Senior Night was very emotional. I cried on the floor. I always said I wouldn't all three years leading up to that, watching guys get all teary-eyed. But seeing my parents up there and knowing that they were unbelievably supportive, coming to all but three games whether the team was playing in Hawaii or North Carolina or L.A. or wherever, they were there. Luckily, they had the means to do that. And there were a lot of times I wasn't playing a lot, and they didn't care. There'd be games where I played five minutes, and they were still there. Seeing them out there and hugging my mom and dad was pretty cool and I'll never, ever forget that. And then again, that's what made that whole day so neat in addition to winning the game and winning the league.

Jeff Boschee

It's kind of hard to pinpoint one special thing concerning KU—basically everything revolved around Kansas basketball my four years playing. I liked the atten-

Jeff Boschee (Lawrence Journal-World)

tion, playing in the big time. The best part for me, coming from a small town in North Dakota, is that I never thought I would get to experience something like this, playing in front of 16,000 people on the floor.

Senior Night was pretty tough. You realize that it's the last time you'll ever set foot in Allen Fieldhouse to play a game or wear a Kansas uniform. You've been there for three years before and you just kind of take it for granted that you'll play another game in the fieldhouse. It finally came to an end, and it was kind of hard to take, sitting there thanking all the coaches and the family and stuff like that. I think the hardest part for me was thanking Coach Williams for just giving me a chance to play here. That's when I got a little bit teary. Thanking my family was pretty tough, too.

Adonis Jordan

That was cool. That was real nice. My mom came up for Senior Night, and they showed me a lot of love. It was very emotional. I remember thinking "Could I get four more years, please?" because it had been so good, my time at KU. I had a lot of fun, learned a lot, grew a lot as a person. Coach Williams definitely instilled a lot of values in me, in the team. He had his own methods, and they worked. It's something I'll never forget.

Nick Bradford

It was a great honor to play at a historic place like KU. The fans and the city and the team—just a great feeling. Knowing that the people back in your hometown watched you play and knowing that you played in one of the top programs in the country was tremendous. The whole

Roy Williams (Lawrence Journal-World)

balance of everything was good. You can go to a lot of places and you don't feel the "family atmosphere," but here, everyone was together, and the former players all come back. You might not even know somebody, but you feel like a part of them because they played at Kansas, played for Coach Williams. It was just a great feeling and something that nobody can take from you.

Tony Guy

KU's a special place. There are a lot of places to go to school in the country, but there aren't too many as special as the University of Kansas. And it's because of the people. I've been with State Farm Insurance for 15 years, and there have been times when I would call Coach Williams and ask him to come and speak at one of our big meetings or something. Now you're talking about a guy for whom I did not play. He said, "Tony, sure. Where at? When?" That's special that KU is the type of place where I can call a coach I did not play for and he says, "No problem." It's the relationships. That guy who's up there right now is exceptional. Those guys are extremely fortunate to be able to play for Roy Williams. He's a special, special man.

Celebrate the Heroes of Kansas and Big 12 Conference Sports

These Other Acclaimed Titles from Sports Publishing!

Kansas City Chiefs Encyclopedia
by Mark Stallard
- 8.5" x 11" hardcover
- 400 pages • photos throughout
- **$39.95**
- 2002 release!

A Salute to Nebraska's Tom Osborne
by the Lincoln Journal Star
- 8.5" x 11" hard/softcover
- 282 pages
- 150+ color and b/w photos
- **$29.95 (hardcover)**
- **$19.95 (softcover)**

Kansas City Chiefs Encyclopedia (leatherbound edition)
by Mark Stallard
- 8.5" x 11" leatherbound
- 400 pages • photos throughout
- **$74.95**

- All copies signed by Art Still, Bill Kenney, Gary Barbaro, Frank Jackson, Carlos Carson, Christian Okoye, Tommy Broker, John Alt, Mike Bell, Mike Livingston, Jan Stenerud, Hank Stram, Bill Maas, and Jim Marsalis!

Bud Wilkinson: An Intimate Portrait of an American Legend
by Jay Wilkinson with Gretchen Hirsch
- 6" x 9" hardcover
- 248 pages • eight-page photo section
- **$19.95**

Tales from Aggieland: Home of the Twelfth Man
by Bo Carter and Mike McKenzie
- 5.5" x 8.25" hardcover
- 200 pages • photos throughout
- **$19.95**
- 2002 release!

George Brett: A Royal Hero
by The Kansas City Star
- 8.5" x 11" hard/softcover
- 204 pages
- 100+ photos
- **$24.95 (hardcover)**
- **$19.95 (softcover)**

Ricky Williams: Dreadlocks to Ditka
by Steve Richardson
- 6" x 9" softcover
- 285 pages
- eight-page photo section
- **$14.95**

The Best of the Big Red Running Backs
by the Lincoln Journal Star
- 8.5" x 11" hardcover
- 169 pages
- 100+ photos
- **$29.95**

To order at any time, please call toll-free **877-424-BOOK (2665)**.
For fast service and quick delivery, order on-line at
www.SportsPublishingLLC.com.